MASTERING
affluence

6 Lessons to Create
a Life You Love

CAROL TUTTLE

Dressing Your Truth®, Energy Profiling®, and Energy Type℠
are trademarks or registered trademarks of
Carol Tuttle Enterprises, LLC.

Library of Congress Control Number: 2018906739
ISBN: 978-0-9844021-1-3

Editing by Kathy West
Cover design by Timothy Kavmark
Text layout by TeaBerry Creative

Live Your Truth Press
support@liveyourtruth.com
liveyourtruth.com

Table of Contents

Before We Begin...

"Within every human being is the natural tendency and capacity to live wholeness [affluence] of life—to be fully awake and aware of the holistic qualities of life while applying all the specific laws of nature to accomplish one's goals.

"It is incomplete development of the human mind that has produced the conception of a normal person as one who makes mistakes, has problems, falls sick, and is at the mercy of circumstances [struggle]. When the total potential of Natural Law is awakened in human awareness, life can be lived in fulfillment, free from mistakes, problems, and illness. Higher states of consciousness and a state of wholeness [affluence] are characterized by complete alertness and spontaneous use of one's full potential: command over one's destiny, with the organizing power to accomplish any worthy goal without strain: a spontaneously nourishing, life-supporting effect on everyone and everything: and the quality of bliss and wholeness [affluence] pervading one's existence."
—*Maharishi University, 1996*

1

Sixteen years ago, I published a book that began with this quotation. Writing that book, *Remembering Wholeness,* was a powerful experience in welcoming a new way of thinking and being into my life. Since publishing *Remembering Wholeness,* countless people have contacted me to say how much of an impact that book had on every aspect of their lives. It opened their minds to the possibility of living free of struggle. They used the principles I wrote about to shift their lives in dramatic ways. Over the years, more than 120,000 copies of that book have sold. It's been a joyous experience to share the lessons I learned with so many people.

In my interactions over the years, I've also noticed that some people who love the freeing principles in *Remembering Wholeness* still remain stuck in certain patterns of struggle that prevent them from fully living with joy and ease. When I wrote the book, I understood the concepts in theory, but I didn't yet know how much greater my capacity was for a life of affluence, ease, and joy. So much more was available to me that I hadn't yet imagined! To varying degrees, people who have read *Remembering Wholeness* understood the concepts, as I did, but haven't fully brought the benefits of those concepts into their life. After interacting with enough people who could use more support to fully practice the teachings of *Remembering Wholeness,* I knew I needed to write more.

If you had a life-changing experience with that book, consider the possibility that even more joy is waiting for you! Some of your lingering patterns may be so conditioned that you don't even see how they keep you from your full potential.

Mastering Affluence is my sequel to *Remembering Wholeness*. Why has it taken me 15 years to write the sequel? I had my own lessons to learn! Once we enroll ourselves in mentally grasping new insights and beliefs, we also enroll the powers of creation in helping us learn the life practice. I've lived out powerful personal lessons in every topic I will discuss in this book, and I will show you how to do the same. *Mastering Affluence* is the practice that helps you take *Remembering Wholeness* to another level, to truly create a life of affluence, ease, and joy. Our souls are ready for different lessons at different times of life. My soul has taken me through the learning necessary to share these lessons with you. You're here, which means you are ready for the next step in living an affluent life.

Consider the possibility that if you apply the teachings and practices I share in this book, that you will not have to go through the experience of learning through pain, as I sometimes did. I believe one of my soul purposes is to share what I learn. I am a teacher. While learning these lessons, I experienced struggles to teach you about, so that you don't have to go through them yourself!

Although some people might define affluence solely as financial wealth, I've found that a truly affluent life is rich in six main areas: spiritual, mental, emotional, physical, financial, and in relationships. If one particular area is lacking or troubled, you feel it, and no amount of money changes that. In this book, I'll guide you through all six areas in a way that helps you clear away patterns of struggle, so that you can bring what you know into practice and create a truly affluent life.

. . .

When I first read that "within every human being is the natural tendency and capacity to live wholeness," I knew that what I read was true. That quote is telling us: We no longer have to accept lack, pain, and struggle as our everyday experience, and if we apply the effort to awaken in ourselves (to remember) a higher state of consciousness and put it into life practices, we can experience affluence, ease, and joy as our new norm. Reading that quote over sixteen years ago was the beginning of my understanding that we have the power to influence our day-to-day experience in a profound way. I knew it was possible to create the experience of wholeness and affluence in my own lifetime.

At that time, accepting this idea as truth was not mainstream, nor was the process of realizing its potential. You might hear people today talk about creating abundance or living at a higher state of consciousness. But sixteen years ago, I never heard people around me talk about these concepts, let alone put them into practice. I knew I had to take my well-being into my own hands and learn how to manifest my own potential for affluence in all areas of my life.

All these years later, I live more fully in the present, I am emotionally and spiritually at peace, I'm the healthiest and wealthiest I've ever been, and I enjoy harmony and partnership in my relationship. Higher consciousness is a journey, not a destination, so I am still learning how to consciously show up in my life in a way that allows affluence, ease, and joy to be constant for me. Every day, I witness evidence that more is possible.

We now live at a time when the choice of affluence has never been more available to us. The irony is, we are also living at a time of high anxiety, tension, and passion, in highly charged political, social, economic, and personal environments. How can the two exist together? We live in a realm of opposition. In other words, we are experiencing more than ever complete opposites in what is available to us. You can easily create a life of suffering, pain, and angst. Or you can make the opposite choice to craft your own experience of well-being and affluence. You have the opportunity to determine the kind of life you want. I'm not saying you have the power to choose every mortal experience. Yet, I do believe you have chosen your experience here at a deeper, unconscious soul level. What you do have complete power over is how you respond to whatever shows up in your mortal experience that feels unchosen. As hierarchical systems continue to fall apart and create more individual freedom, your well-being lies in your own hands more than ever.

Learning how to become a master of your own well-being allows you to consistently create and experience affluence, ease, and joy in all areas of your life. What it requires does not take a lot of time out of your day. Rather, it requires that you become aware of the nuances of your habits. Whatever compromises your potential for well-being is found in the cracks and crevices of your day-to-day choices and familiar patterns. Your daily patterns are so conditioned that you may not even recognize the small ways you're limiting yourself. Once you learn how, creating a life of affluence does not take any more time or effort than creating a life of struggle.

We each have inherent in us all the capacity to create lives of affluence, ease, and joy. We are just bringing forth the recollection, the memory that we hold deep in our God-given design of how to do it. We came to this earth embodying the potential to create lives of wholeness and affluence. It is our opportunity to call forth and activate that intelligence of affluence we each carry.

Imagine a world where disease is a choice. Imagine a world where everyone has the money they need with extra to spare to support their interests, desires, and purpose. Imagine a world where parents raise children to be civil-minded adults who choose to serve and make a difference. Imagine a world where human beings know who they are and live in alignment with their highest good. Imagine a world where peace presides.

What else can you imagine? What do you want to create?

6 Lessons, 6 Areas of Affluence

I had to personally learn the practice of creating affluence in all six areas I address in this book: spiritual, mental, emotional, physical, financial, and in relationship. I have experienced spiritual doubt and confusion, mental depression and torment, deep emotional wounding, chronic physical pain, crippling financial debt, and a turbulent and difficult intimate relationship with my husband. I have successfully changed all six areas from a state of lack, pain, and struggle to experiences of affluence, ease, and joy—all by daily practice of what I teach in the six lessons in this book. My learning does not come by scientific study of how to create a life of affluence. I am a teacher of the practical and my life has been my laboratory. My life is the proof in the pudding.

I frequently receive thank you notes from people all over the world who are students of my work who share similar stories as Rebecca:

> "Thank you, Carol. From studying your teachings and putting them to practice, I have experienced healing from a long-term illness and every aspect of my life has improved, from my health, marriage and my experience as a parent. Thank you for showing me how to create an affluent life."

In this book, you will find powerful truths about affluence, as well as stories from a few of the thousands of individuals I've been able to help over the years. As you practice the principles in this book, you can experience your own powerful story, too.

IMPORTANT: This book is meant to be used and practiced.

Just skimming through the chapters will *not* bring as much change as you are seeking! The life-changing effects of this book are only available if you put the principles into practice. For that reason, I encourage you to follow the guidance I've set out for you. Here's how to get amazing results.

Mastering Affluence is written in two parts. Part One, Choosing Affluence, helps you gain a clearer understanding of what affluence truly is and how you are resisting it. In Part One, you will recognize current patterns that keep you living in the range of suffering to mediocrity. I'll introduce you to the six areas of affluence in depth, so that you have a clear picture of what's possible—and which areas of your life are still stuck in lack, pain, and struggle. Our habits of living in a compromised state can be so developed that we don't even notice. Reading Part One will help you recognize where you're compromised that you don't realize.

Part Two, Creating Affluence, is the practice. The main reason you still experience lack, pain, and struggle is not because you don't know better. You do it mostly out of habit. You make invisible, automatic choices in what you think, the beliefs you still sustain (both consciously and unconsciously), and the emotions that you run. When you are living in lack, pain, and struggle, these choices compound your beliefs and create more of what you don't want in life.

Part Two is organized in six lessons, one for each area of affluence. Making lasting change in all areas of your life is too big a task to do all at once! I've broken down the pieces and practices into steps that you can manage and maintain. These six lessons guide you through a journey of self-accountability to put into practice new choices and new habits. Over time, your life will continuously shift from one of lack, pain, and struggle to one of greater affluence, ease, and joy.

You will experience remarkable and immediate shifts by putting into practice what you learn. To maintain those shifts and turn them into your consistent life experience, you need to practice. The patterns of lack, pain, and struggle have been acquired through generations that preceded you. Like me, you may be the first person in your family line who has consciously made the choice to create something different. Congratulations on choosing to create a life of affluence, ease, and joy! I am here to show you the way. I've made it my life practice to apply the strategies and principles I will teach you. I use them every day.

Start thinking about which areas of your life you would like to experience more affluence, ease, and joy in. You will have opportunities to make those changes while you are reading this book. Be glad those opportunities are showing up for you. Trust that your life is playing out perfectly for you. You already have the roadmap to a life of affluence within you. This book will help you bring that map to light so you can create a life that you love. Let's get started!

PART ONE

Choosing Affluence

The challenge of our time is no longer how much pain you can endure. Our new challenge is: How big can you dream? How much joy can you hold? And how long will you let it be that way?

What Is Affluence?

Most people would reduce their definition of affluence to an experience with money, as if just having a lot of money creates an affluent life. Yes, money is part of an affluent life, but only a part.

- Affluence is first a state of being—an inner state of knowing all is well, and life is playing out perfectly for you.

- Affluence starts in the inner realm of who we are, and then is experienced as our outer reality.

- Affluence is an ability to maintain a state of peace and happiness, regardless of life's outer circumstances. It is mastery over the inner self. It is as though your soul's knowing has awakened and is now incarnate in your physical reality. As this awakening occurs in your inner experience of self, your outer reality transforms in many ways to reflect back to you a life free of lack, pain, and struggle.

In your physical reality, affluence is the condition of abundance in your passions, desires, and those things that help you fulfill your soul purpose. Affluence in your physical world looks like having enough and more of what supports a blessed and blissful existence.

Affluence is moving through challenges with a peaceful knowing that you are being guided and led each step of the way, that God is with you and by you.

Many people question me on the concept of living a life free of struggle. In fact, some people have debated me so strongly, they seem to defend struggle itself. The typical belief behind someone's passion to believe in a life of struggle is: We need it. There is this idea that if we don't struggle, we will all turn into ungrateful slobs who are lazy and apathetic about life. In other words, they believe we need struggle to keep us on our toes and on our knees, in order to keep us humble.

I will admit that struggle and pain have been great teachers! They definitely have sent me to my knees hundreds of times throughout my life. But over twenty years ago, the scripture John 15:11 caused me to question this collective belief in "struggle" as being necessary and as the norm.

"I have told you this so that my joy may be in you and that your joy may be complete." —John 15:11

At a conference I attended recently, one of the presenters on a panel fielded a question about struggling in life. He is a well-known blogger with a rich and affluent life. His answer was, "I don't believe in struggle. Struggle is a human creation." Several of the other panelists were thrown by his answer. One of them looked at him and declared, "I believe you have to have struggle if you're going to progress," and a number of people in the audience gave him a big cheer! If we depend on struggle in order to progress, then of course we will create the experience of struggle for ourselves.

Affluence starts in your inner being, with your beliefs, thoughts, and feelings. When you choose to live an affluent life, you make choices based on a deep belief that you can progress while thriving. If you hold that belief consistently over time, you will find that your external circumstances align for that to be true for you. You can hold onto your belief in the need for struggle if you want to. But you've read this far, which means you're ready to let go of old beliefs and live the affluent life that is waiting for you.

If your focus is on the negative, then you will experience life as getting harder. If your focus is on the positive, you will experience life as getting easier.

What Is the Difference Between Affluence and Abundance?

I went back and forth on whether I should title this book *Mastering Affluence* or *Creating Abundance*. The word *abundance* has grown popular in the past several years as the consciousness movement hit a mass audience.

When you think of the word *abundance,* what comes to mind? An abundance of money is often the most common reference. Abundance can also include a reference to a life of luxury, fine personal belongings, and in some cases, also include health or relationships. Abundance is often thought of as an end result, rather than the means to an end.

I decided to go against the pop culture of the consciousness movement and choose the word *affluence.* Let me explain why.

The word *abundance* refers to "a very large quantity of something." The truth is, you are ALWAYS creating abundance. You are a creator in the midst of a system of creation called the Universe that is always set on the *abundance* setting. You cannot create a lack of anything. You are consistently creating an abundance of whatever you focus on. Where your thoughts and feelings are focused, that is where your energy flows. And where your energy flows, you create more of the same. If you are focused on too much debt, you will create an abundance of debt. If you are focused on poor health and physical pain, you will create an abundance of poor health and physical pain. If you are focused on how hard your relationships are, you will create an abundance of painful challenges in your relationships.

I purposely chose the word *affluence* to differentiate from *abundance*. In this book, the word *affluence* refers to a state of having a lot of what is desired to experience a joy-filled life—perfectly designed for you to manifest into existence. The spiritual blueprint for your life of affluence—uniquely designed for you—already exists. Your job is to help it come into material manifestation.

If we have a spiritual blueprint for lives of affluence, ease, and joy, why do we not just automatically create this as our experience in life? We stay stuck because of generational patterns that precede us in the form of thoughts and feelings, as well as patterns of lack, pain, and struggle modeled to us as we grow up. Those patterns become our beliefs, our perceptions of the world, and the language we use. As you shift and stop the patterns of lack, pain, and struggle that were handed down from generations before, you bring your blueprint of affluence into your life. You advance the potential to create lives of affluence, ease, and joy into the posterity of your family system—without them even knowing what you are up to.

Look at your life. What have you created an abundance of? It could be inner peace. It could be inner turmoil. Maybe you've created an abundance of money or an abundance of debt. What you focus on comes to you in abundance. It's no trick to create abundantly—we cannot do otherwise. What *does* take practice and careful attention is creating affluence. And that's what I'm here to help you do.

Rather than focus on what IS in your world,
focus on what you want your world to be.

Affluence is Our Birthright

The opposites of affluence are lack, pain, and struggle. Lack, pain, and struggle are familiar experiences for many people today, yet I do not believe they are our natural state.

Our natural God-given state is one of affluence, ease, and joy. If lack, pain, and struggle were our natural state, we'd just be okay with those experiences and not make any efforts to improve the quality of our lives. We would know and feel at peace with the belief that life is hard, it is difficult most of the time, and you need to just learn to survive and accept it because that is what we came to mortality to experience. We would basically be okay with lives of struggle and mediocrity. We are not okay with struggle, though, which is a message for us.

Struggle is an experience we create in this life. It's not good or bad, right or wrong; it's an experience. We are meant to live in ease and joy. You're here, reading this book, which means you're ready to let go of the struggle and live the life of affluence that is possible for you.

We appear to be very close to making space travel an option to consumers who can afford to invest in the experience of going into outer space. It's time we explored our inner space to open our potential for living in affluence on all levels. Our souls are here to guide us in that exploration.

Are You Spiritualizing Lack, Pain, and Struggle?

In the archives of religious belief, you can find the origin of the belief that lack, pain, and struggle are all witnesses of spiritual devotion. This was birthed at the time of our ancestors, who made choices that required sacrifice and suffering to obtain religious freedom. Nearly every person has this old belief energy embedded in their subconscious belief system.

We also have a tendency to spiritualize struggle when we believe we can't stop the pain we are experiencing. The mind needs to see some purpose or value in order to endure it.

If you have ever said or were taught, "You grow more spiritual when times are hard," you have set up a pattern that will create times to be hard, in order to evolve spiritually and feel close to God.

Lack, pain, and struggle are old and outdated human conditions. We now have enough resources and knowledge to create a level of comfort and affluence for all of humanity.

The current distribution of resources is not balanced, but as the collective consciousness continues to shift from patterns of lack, pain, and struggle to a consciousness of affluence, ease, and joy, we will continue to be moved to make changes over time that create more balance of resources for all of humanity to benefit from.

Are you still spiritualizing lack, pain, and struggle in your life? Where have you accepted that a condition of struggle is necessary to keep you humble and submissive to God's will? What if you consciously choose God's will, choose to be humble, choose to be obedient to God's will for you? One of the most famous sayings of Jesus may come to mind: "It is easier for a camel to fit through the eye of a needle than for a rich person to enter the Kingdom of Heaven."—Matt. 19:24 (Also found in the Bible in Mark 10:25 and Luke 18:25.)

As I have pondered this scripture, I believe that it is telling us that it is a rare experience to be both rich and humble, affluent and obedient, as this has not been the common practice. It takes a more conscious effort to be submissive and humble to God's will if we are not compelled to be that way. It takes a conscious daily intention to live a life of purpose led by the spirit. To me, mastering affluence requires this deep quality of being both rich and humble, thriving in all areas of your life and being led by the spirit, no longer needing struggle and pain to humble you and bring you to submission. Sounds good to me!

Here's a more light-hearted example. I love these lines in the movie, *Dumb and Dumber*, between Lloyd and Mary:

Lloyd: What do you think the chances are of a guy like me and a girl like you...ending up together?
Mary: Not good.

Lloyd: You mean, not good like one out of a hundred?
Mary: I'd say more like one out of a million.
Lloyd: So you're telling me there's a chance. Yeah![i]

The odds meant nothing to Lloyd. He didn't look at the million. He looked at the one and decided that would be him. Many might say Lloyd is just stupid. But his lines say to me that he focused his energy on the tiniest positive possibility. We smile when he says what he does because he expresses powerful optimism that not many people have.

You can choose to birth yourself from the collective energy of lack, pain, and struggle to create a life of affluence, ease, and joy. You can also choose to be humble and live in the energy of grace. Doing both is equivalent to going through the eye of the needle. It's a less-worn path, but it's possible. As more people choose the eye of the needle, the way is opened for even more to choose that path. Remember: what you need to succeed is first to believe that there is a chance!

Struggles deplete us, challenges feed us.

Opposition in All Things

I am often presented with inquiries from students and clients from various religious practices who have drawn the conclusion that struggle represents a form of opposition that is necessary for our growth. For example, I have received a question along these lines many times:

> Carol, could you touch on the idea of opposition in all things, that we must experience lack, pain, and struggle in order to know things like affluence and joy?

Having been an active member of my own religious affiliation for many years, I had to come to my own answer to understand what opposition really means.

> Opposition to me means what it says: there are opposites in the world. In opposition to light, we have darkness. For cold, we have hot. For good, we have evil. We have opposing experiences and opposing energies to choose from. For us to know the opposite does not mean we have to choose it or live it. We just have to be aware of it.

Which experience do you want? Which energy do you want to live in?

A student of mine shared with me this great explanation of opposition:

> *"Opposition exists to show contrast. If red were the only color available, we wouldn't know what green or blue or yellow are. You don't have to wear those colors to know they exist. You don't have to exist in a state of struggle to know it exists. God wants us to have joy. If bad things didn't exist we wouldn't know we were happy. Some say you have to experience unhappiness to experience happiness. I believe it is enough to simply know it exists."*

In my work with energy healing, I teach that states of happiness are high-vibration states of being and states of unhappiness are low-vibration states. Opposites. We have the agency to choose which state of being we want to experience.

Have you believed you have to personally experience struggle in order to experience joy? What is something in your life that you would like to change, but you have believed you had to learn to live with because you needed opposition? Have you ever thought or made the comment, "I have to learn to live with this?" Consider the possibility that your soul chose this experience as a lesson for you to learn what you really want—the opposite of what you are experiencing now.

Choosing Challenges Rather Than Allowing Struggles

We can be forced to grow through unexpected struggles that cause us to reach deep within and grow beyond our current belief, or we can consciously choose challenges to support us in growing and developing as human beings. What if you could take the same energy that manifests as struggles and consciously choose to create the experience of challenges instead? When I realized I had this option years ago, I started running marathons. I chose to run my first marathon in 2001.

What feels impossible to you? I believed that running 26.2 miles was impossible for me. Even considering this task was overwhelming and struck me with fear. I was not a runner, and to this day, I really don't like running! I chose this experience at a time in my life when I was tired of living life as a victim, feeling powerless against my outside world. I chose to show myself that the impossible was possible. I knew deep in my heart that if I could successfully run a marathon, I would change my worldview and perception of what I believed was possible for myself. It took me eight months to train and build the strength and capacity to run my first marathon.

I remember the day I crossed that finish line. It was one of the greatest spiritual moments that I have ever experienced. I chose to consciously take on a challenge and even induce discomfort to bring to light my disbelief about what I believed was possible—and I overcame it. You can consciously choose your challenges, rather than use ongoing struggles to promote your personal growth. Growing through a challenge you consciously chose involves much more reward and personal satisfaction.

I have come to the conclusion that we are meant to have challenges—and it is up to us if they become struggles. Challenges are a part of this mortal life. They are life situations that call us up to look within, believe in ourselves, ask questions to seek answers, build confidence, and enroll us in accomplishing more than we think we can accomplish. But when we turn our challenges into struggles, we suffer and we have a tendency to feel like victims of life rather than victors.

The truth is, our souls want us to grow. Your soul, your true self, loves a challenge. If you're living in lack, pain, and struggle in any area of your life, consider that the current struggles in your life are an invitation to shift into living a life of affluence. One of my favorite authors, Michael Brown, who wrote *The Presence Process*, teaches that our upsets are a "set-up."[ii] Your soul is setting you up to get your attention so you start to inquire and seek answers to learn differently. Consider the possibility that your current upset was a "set up" that brought you to this book.

How can you take the energy of struggle that keeps materializing in your life and consciously choose a challenge to provoke your growth instead? What is something that you really,

really want to pursue, but have been too afraid to pursue? Use consciously crafted challenges to feed you rather than allowing drama, disharmony, and struggles that deplete you. How long have you been standing at the edge of the water? It's time to sail beyond your current reality, as you perceive it. Your affluent self is calling you to make this journey to creating your truth.

What are you being called to do that seems impossible and way out of your current comfort zone? Decide to do it in the immediate future. Rather than overwhelm yourself and talk yourself out of it by considering all the steps required to take on this challenge, ask God what is your next correct step. As you are shown the next correct step, take it. Then ask again, what is the next step? Then take that step. As you do this, you will build confidence and create momentum to keep moving toward successfully completing this challenge.

The new challenge humanity has is to create a life experience of affluence, ease, and joy. We tend to think that living in lack, pain, and struggle is our challenge. It is not! It is uncomfortable and it is familiar. We are actually very good at it. It is the default mode of humanity as it has been the practice for so many centuries. The old belief of "no pain, no gain" is outdated and ineffective. The new belief of, "I joyously create and celebrate the affluence of my life," is the new challenge. Living this new belief is an unfamiliar experience, yet learning to do so is aligned with our soul purpose.

Living beneath your potential as a creator of your reality causes emotional discomfort. Consider the possibility that you may have altered your expectations of what you believe is possible in an attempt to relieve this discomfort. Altering your expectations does not work over the long term. You continue to feel discomfort with living below your potential and accepting mediocrity as your norm. Do not confuse that discomfort with feeling "challenge," as if settling for mediocrity is something you need to learn how to do better! The truth is you are really, really good at sacrifice and survival! How good are you at receiving and flourishing? Your current discomfort is meant to provoke you to be engaged in a new experience, which is creating a life experience of affluence, ease, and joy.

If there are challenges going on in your life, that means learning is occurring, and where there is learning, there is growing and your soul is guiding you along the way.

Why Your Soul Wants
You to Be Affluent

One of our biggest guiding forces in our lives is our own souls. Our souls know better and recognize the lie we live. I believe your soul holds the blueprint for your affluent life. I believe it is possible to bring forth the quality of your soul's knowing and a remembrance of your soul's truth in your lifetime. As you live out your soul purpose, you experience a sense of confidence that comes from living according to your inner knowing.

When did you last ask or seek to know your soul's purpose?

This is a common quest in today's experience with people who are students of higher consciousness—to know and live your soul purpose.

It's a common conclusion that a soul purpose has a lot to do with a role or a function we play out in our life. It's something we do that makes a difference in the world. Yes, that is definitely a part of your soul purpose. Consider the possibility that it also includes more than that. As I have sought to understand our soul purpose, I have come to realize that it is threefold.

Our souls want us to:

1. Learn specific lessons we came here to learn.
2. Experience what the earthly world has to offer.
3. Give service and make a contribution, using our gifts and talents.

I believe that our souls choose to come into this mortal human experience for these three primary reasons. All three functions of your soul purpose are helped by having financial affluence. I see the role of financial affluence as a tool, a resource to allow you to more fully realize and experience your threefold purpose, which supports you in abundantly creating affluence in all areas of your life. Let's look at our three-fold soul purpose more closely.

1. Lessons to Learn

The lessons I am referring to are life lessons that I believe were chosen by our soul before we entered our mortal experience. We were born into the lesson of learning how to survive and grow from a place of struggle. Our new lessons include learning to grow and thrive in the energy and experience of joy.

To invite the lessons you are meant to learn in this lifetime, here's a good question to ask: "What lessons am I meant to learn?"

Asking yourself this question allows your energy to present itself and differentiate your own energy from your family story. What are your individual lessons? Ask yourself that and the lessons and answers will present themselves.

It's common for people to hesitate to ask this question, as they have a belief that all life lessons involve pain and hardship. That may have been true for a portion of your life, but does not need to be the theme moving forward. What if your lessons involve learning how to receive more? What if they involve learning how to give from the abundant supply of financial affluence you created? What if your lessons include creating a business, starting a non-profit that makes a difference in the world, healing a physical condition you once believed you could never change? Mastering the experience of partnership in a loving and collaborative relationship? So many life lessons can be birthed from the energy of joy. Which lessons of joy are waiting to be learned in your lifetime?

2. Experiences to Have

I believe that as souls, we chose to come into this earth life to have experiences. I don't mean the experiences related to the lessons we are learning. By experiences, I mean the act of becoming more aware, more conscious, and more awake to what we are experiencing. It's important to be aware of the power we have to create our experience. I believe there are both experiences our soul feels called to have and experiences that would just feel enjoyable and pleasurable to us.

Ask yourself the following questions to initiate the manifestation of what you came to experience in your lifetime:

- Which experiences am I meant to have in my lifetime?
- What are my life goals and dreams?

37

- What did I come to experience in the physical realm?
- Which foods do I want to taste?
- What relationships do I want to enjoy?
- How do I want to experience my physical body and its form?
- Which talents am I meant to develop?
- How do I want to use my talents, behaviors, and personality to pursue a career path?
- Where do I want to travel?
- What expressions of nature do I want to explore and experience?

Experiences can include a job that is fulfilling and materially supporting. When we are in balance with a profession we love that allows us to make a contribution through our work (and we receive an abundance of money in return), we create more options for ourselves to choose more experiences. Creating financial affluence is a worthy pursuit, as money is a tool to create the experiences we want.

3. Service to Give

When you're living in affluence, you're able to give service to others. Instead of walking around thinking, *I don't have enough time, money, or love to give to anyone else,* you live your life knowing there is enough time, love, and money to serve others.

In my book, *It's Just My Nature,* and through much of the content on my website, I teach the model of Energy Profiling. This model teaches that everyone moves through life in a unique way. For instance, some people express themselves in an animated way, while others are more reserved. Some people jump into action, while others are more methodical. I call these patterns of movement the four Energy Types. You are a combination of all four movements, but you dominantly express one particular Energy Type throughout your life.

When we live authentically to our own specific Energy Type, we are able to serve others with integrity. Living in energetic alignment makes it easier to serve while respecting yourself and others. For instance, my Energy Type is characterized by a determined, forward drive that moves things into action. A couple of decades ago, someone I had turned to for guidance and support shared with me: "Your energy is like a plow. You pave the way, you are a path maker. The paths you make are like a highway for others to travel." And just recently, in an online course I taught, a woman thanked me for being a snowplow that all the participants could ski behind. I recognize that one of the ways I serve others is to pioneer the fields of consciousness. Creating pathways, supporting humanity by snowplowing a smoother path for others, is one of my soul's purposes and it's authentic to my Energy Type. When I embrace that quality in myself, I am able to serve others around me naturally, just by being myself. By living true to yourself, you can serve others, too.

(If you haven't yet heard of Energy Profiling or discovered your Energy Type, see the appendix at the back of this book. I've created many resources to help you identify your Energy Type and live true to who you really are.)

As you look for opportunities to serve, the Universe will create them. As you seek to know who you might serve and how, your soul will tell you.

In *Remembering Wholeness*, I wrote, "When you give someone love and support, you give yourself love and support."[iii] What we give to others in time, talents, or resources comes back to us at least tenfold.

What service are you meant to give to others? As you pose this question, you activate the energy for life to show to you the unique opportunities that you have to serve and contribute from your authentic self. As you serve from your authentic self, the energy you put out as service returns to you multiplied and serves you.

Affluence is not something we acquire, it is something we awaken to. As we awaken the energy of affluence in us, our world reflects it back to us.

What Affluence Looks Like
in Our Day-to-Day Lives

You have two experiences to your world: your inner world and your outer world. Your inner world is your connection to your spiritual source and your soul (your spiritual body), your thinking mind (your mental body), and your feelings (your emotional body). Your outer world consists of your physical self (your physical body), and health, money, and relationships—the three areas of our outer world where we create the most lack, pain, and struggle. So altogether, you have the opportunity each day to create affluence in your spiritual, mental, and emotional experience, and in your health, money, and relationships. Let's look at what affluence can look like in each of these six areas.

Your Inner World

The average human is primarily focused on their outer world experience because that is what they interact with every day. People tend not to go inward if things are going smoothly. We go along, focusing on our outer world, until something draws us within and requires us to seek answers and insights to better our outer world circumstances and help us shift from lack, pain, and struggle to affluence, ease, and joy in both the inner and outer world.

Going inward was always your soul's design. We live at a time when our "inner eyes," or insight, are being opened. Creating an affluent inner world is the first step to mastering affluence in your outer world, as the outer world is a reflection of the inner world.

> Realty is the relationship of the internal world with the
> external world, producing a standing wave that produces
> the reality we see around us.
>
> —*Nassim Naramein*

Your inner world has an energetic hierarchy that is created by three energetic fields of expression: your spiritual, mental, and emotional experiences with yourself.

Your spiritual energy body or energy field is the highest vibration of you. You can only know truth in this field of energy. God and your soul connect to you through the spiritual energy plane. This energy holds the blueprint for your true self and your affluent life. There is never any need to heal your spiritual energy field, as no one can damage it. This could be a reason why some people have withstood the horrors of humanity. The likes of Victor Frankl and Anne Frank could be considered two humans who had active, strong connections with their spiritual energy field and access to truth which helped them withstand and overcome great tragedies in their life. Each of us has the opportunity to develop a strong connection to our spiritual energy, to activate the blueprint of our true selves, and to manifest the reality of spiritual affluence in our lives.

The next highest vibration of your inner world is your mental energy field. This is the thinking mind, where you experience your thoughts. You are always thinking. We experience the constant "yapping" of a voice inside of us. What is it saying? Is it repeating thoughts that aren't even yours? Is it saying nice things and constructive things about you?

We now move to your emotional energy field, where you feel your feelings. This is a field of energy that we are learning to pioneer for a healthy expression of emotion. Unhealthy expression of emotion has been pent up for generations of humanity and we can see its results in the world all around us. As we learn to release layers of pent-up negative emotion, we free ourselves and the collective energy of humanity to experience more joy and peace as our natural state of being. We are wired to be kind, civil, happy people when we have access to a healthy emotional energy field.

As we heal and cleanse the emotional and mental energy fields, spiritual energy then flows more readily and fully into these two other bodies of energy in our inner world.

Let's take a closer look at what affluence looks and feels like in your inner world. We'll look at each of these energetic expressions of self: spiritual, mental, and emotional.

What is Spiritual Affluence?

Affluence begins in the spiritual energy field. It is a personal experience that is often private.

People often combine spirituality and religion. I will clarify here that I experience spirituality as a different experience than religiosity. Spirit energy is our private and personal experience with God and the heavens. Spirituality is our inner connection to the Divine and to our soul. The inner experience of spirituality is built right into our collective human experience. You have access to truth in your spiritual energy. You just have to bring that truth to life within you, so that it becomes your familiar experience.

Religiosity is the outer practice of expressing and practicing our inner spirituality in an organized format of worshiping the Divine. Religion offers us the opportunity to come together in community to practice our chosen religion and to worship as we believe.

As we awaken to our unique experience of spiritual affluence, the energy is shifting. Previously, an outside ecclesiastical source defined for us what and how to worship. We are shifting from that outer experience to an inner guidance awakening in us, creating our own personal experience of spirituality, and defining the ways we choose to express that inner spirituality in our outer world.

Some people can be challenged by this shift, as not everyone is going through it at the same time. People who choose spirituality without religion may misjudge people who choose to practice within religious experiences. People within a religious practice may misjudge those who choose not to participate. Even within communities of religious worship, we can witness a range of experiences. I've learned to trust that everyone is on their own path and to respect that. As I have awakened to my own understanding of the Divine, I recognize that not everyone is having my experience, nor are they even meant to.

Let's look at two examples of this shift taking place, with two different outcomes influenced by their early religious experiences. We'll call these examples Sam and Sue. You may relate to one of their stories.

Sam was raised in an organized religion with a strict approach. His parents dictated how to worship God and what was right and wrong, according to the leaders of their religion. Sam was not given support to explore his own spirituality and define his religious experience for himself. He was told what he should and shouldn't do. As his own spiritual awakening occurred, he asked questions. These questions were threatening to his parents and seen as a sign of disbelief in what they had worked so hard to teach him. Sam found no room for personal exploration and interpretation of his own spirituality, based on what his parents had shown him, so he left his religion in order to experience the freedom of spiritual self-expression.

In another scenario, Sue was raised in a religious family. Her parents taught her principles and practices they believed to be true according to their religion, and encouraged her to know for herself what she believed. She was encouraged to ask questions, explore her spirituality, and find answers independent of her parents and ecclesiastical leaders. Sue has chosen to stay involved with her religious community and continues to find it a supportive place to experience her own personal spirituality.

Both individuals were a part of the same religious group, with different outcomes. As we continue this shift from top-down religiosity to more personalized spirituality, it's important that we allow others space to have their own experience.

Our spiritual energy is powerful and it is awakening to our own personal connection with God and our soul. Trust the process as you are guided in awakening and accessing your spiritual affluence.

Spiritual affluence goes beyond your practice of formally worshiping the Divine. You can notice it is developing for you through simple things. You may be driving or walking on a clear day and suddenly notice how much more vivid the colors are, or you may feel a greater sense of internal peacefulness and quiet.

As you are awakening to your spiritual affluence, what spiritual epiphanies do you have? What spiritual moments are you reverencing? What's happening for you spiritually that you can identify as your affluence, ease, and joy?

What is Mental Affluence?

As we move down the energetic hierarchy of the inner realm, we come to the inner experience of our thinking mind—the mental energy field. The vibration of the mental plane is a slower vibration than the spiritual energy plane, but it is one of the most dominant influences in our lives and has a stronghold on our planet: the mind thinks it's king! Many leaders of the consciousness movement have helped us understand how to make our minds our servants, rather than us being the servant of the mind. Eckhart Tolle's teachings of presence and the power of living in the now and Byron Katie's process called *The Work* both help us learn to train our minds to serve our spirits.[iv]

I became a student of a mindfulness practice when I attended a 21-day silent retreat in southern India in 2010. I was on a remote campus in Southern India that housed about 200 students for 21 days. We did experience daily meditations and lectures, but the main goal was to not speak for 21 days in order to learn our mind's habits and start breaking down the mental power our minds can keep us locked in. We lived in dorms of about 14 people of the same gender and we spent time around people all day. Most of the students could not go for more than three to four days without speaking and would have to be reminded to enroll themselves in the practice of silence again. Approximately 25 students of the 200 were able to be silent for 21 consecutive days. I knew the chance was very slim that I would be in a position again to choose this experience. I had invested a significant amount of money and flown halfway around the world to have this experience, so I took it seriously! I was one of those students who maintained silence for the full retreat. I am grateful I chose to maintain silence, as I learned so much about my thinking mind that still serves me today. It's not likely that you will enroll yourself in a silent retreat for 21 days (though you might!). But you can still begin to develop mindfulness practices that give you the tools you need to start quieting your mind. In Part Two of this book, I will introduce you to some practices and offer you some exercises to quiet your mind and allow your soul's voice to guide your life. Here are some of the lessons I learned to get you started:

WHAT I LEARNED FROM MY SILENT RETREAT

The mind is noisy! In the first few days of silence, the mind starts to go crazy with a lot of inner chatter. It gets noisy inside and you wish you had a switch to turn it off!

After the first week, the mind starts to get quiet and the inner world becomes very peaceful. There was nothing I had to think about, and nowhere I had to be but with myself. Another practice at the retreat was to not be connected online, so I basically had no interaction with the outside world I had left behind.

By week two, I began to be an observer of my mind, rather than feeling one with my thinking mind. I was able to watch my thoughts and feel as if they were something streaming through me, rather than something I was consciously choosing to think. The mind likes to stay busy with one thought after another and another and another. The analytical mind wants to run your life and thinks it knows best. But I discovered it doesn't always know the best choices. I learned that the thinking mind was a great tool to help me manage tasks in my life, such as getting the laundry done, and helping me know what I had to remember to follow through on. Yet it was not the best source to guide my life and help me develop my spiritual knowing.

By week three, I began to experience space between the thoughts, which created a quiet and peaceful state of mind. This is an interesting state to be in, as you can interpret it as boredom, as if there is not enough going on inside of you. Yet, with enough practice, you can create a new habit of going within to a quiet space of the self.

By being silent for 21 days, I began to hear the inner voice of my higher self, the conscious part of me. I began to learn and understand that the energy of the thinking mind is one big network that everyone is plugged into. It is one of the strongest energy fields that humanity is connected with. I learned that higher consciousness is different from the thinking mind. The thinking mind can be trained. As you love your mind, it responds to your efforts to shift into being a tool, rather than a power that runs your life.

In the end, 21 days of not talking is actually a big relief. I realized that we spend most of our lives looking outside of ourselves, distracting ourselves. Not speaking for 21 days induces a multi-day meditation where the focus shifts from the outer world to the inner self. It's a safe and peaceful place to be once the noise quiets down.

....

A mind that thinks in an affluent way is trained to serve you. An affluent mind is an affirmative mind rather than a suffering mind. I've trained my mind to see myself, my world, and my experiences as supportive.

As you learn to have an affirmative mind, you will more readily create a life of affluence, ease, and joy.

Do you regularly think about affluence, ease, and joy? What's going on for you mentally? How much peace and stillness do you experience in your own head? Do you have increasing, expanding joy and ease in your thoughts? Are you consciously choosing not to suffer anymore? Do you perceive the world as one that supports you? Do you expect joyful experiences?

What is Emotional Affluence?

The third energy field of the inner self is the emotional energy field. Only in the last several decades has the emotional energy field been activated and actively pioneered.

Our ancestors were focused primarily on meeting their physical needs and their emotional experience was less of a priority. Sure, people have allowed their emotional energy to fuel their choices in many cases, but we have not been students of this powerful energy until the 1970s, when the recovery movement started for children who were taught not to feel their feelings. Since that time, we have gone from recovery to healing to spiritual awakening to the emotional shifts that humanity has been going through for the last 40-50 years. Only recently have we understood that we all carry a degree of buried emotion that was passed on to us by our ancestors and overlooked from our childhood.

Emotional affluence is a state of inner wellbeing, with an inner sense of overriding peace. It's a sense of reassurance that everything is okay in our lives. This emotional state is not dependent on outside circumstances. We certainly can allow our emotional feathers to be ruffled, due to outside circumstances, but in a state of emotional affluence, we still feel an inner current of peace and harmony that is constant. This is not achieved overnight or even within months. It can take years of practice to develop this emotional state. The key is clearing the underlying feelings inherited from past generations, or the repressed childhood emotions that are muddled in our emotional energy body that continue to get triggered and stirred up. Consider the possibility that any overly charged emotion that is disruptive to your inner peace is repressed from an early time in your life and is asking for you to clear it from your emotional body.

Gratitude is one of the highest vibrations of emotional affluence. Expressing gratitude for where your affluence, ease, and joy are showing up puts you in a cycle that allows you to manifest more things for which to be grateful.

To achieve a state of emotional affluence requires us to pioneer our emotional energy body—to go within and feel our feelings. The baby boomer generation included certain pioneers of the emotional plane. Those of us who felt called to do this work sought to be free of emotional pain. We discovered that we had to go within, learn to feel our feelings, and no longer repress our emotional energy that otherwise would manifest in our bodies as physical disease. For many of us of this generation, Louise Hay was the original Lewis and Clark of the emotional energy plane.

She was one of the few authors of her time to pave the path and to give us headlamps on our emotional journey. She taught us that emotional energy can turn into physical imbalance and disease. These ideas were new when she published her first book, *You Can Heal Your Life.*[v] They have now been backed by more and more scientific evidence that our emotions affect our physical health.[vi]

I started my emotional healing in 1985 by studying the teachings of John Bradshaw and learning to do inner-child healing strategies. At this time, I became aware of unexpressed buried emotions from my childhood and ancestral emotional inheritance. In my parents' generation and earlier, you didn't feel your feelings. Children at that time were not acknowledged for their emotional expression. Emotion was quickly shamed, disciplined, or punished.

In pioneering your emotional energy, you will learn to be the parent of feelings that were not recognized and honored in your childhood. You will also feel what has been repressed throughout your life and honor your emotional energy, so it doesn't get the best of you and turn into inappropriate behavior that you act out toward yourself or others.

If you are someone like me, who has been doing emotional healing work for years or even decades, you may have asked yourself this question:

"When does the emotional healing process come to an end?
I have been doing healing work for years already."

Our mind thinks we are trying to get to a destination or get a job done. When you begin to heal your life's emotional patterns of lack, pain, and struggle, you start the process of thinking, *I am going to get to a place where I am free of this.* We'll talk more about this pattern in Part Two, where I will help you get unstuck from that frustration. Until then, know that emotional healing is your evolution. As you emotionally heal, you evolve, and as you heal you wake up to your true feelings of emotional affluence. As you clean up your emotional energy and release the repressed emotion of your childhood, you are free to feel your true state of emotional affluence.

When we start on the path to healing our patterns of lack, pain, and struggle, we can commonly overlook emotional energy. Outer issues such as physical health, painful relationships, or lack of money tend to enroll us first. Whatever form of lack, pain and struggle has shown up for you, it's getting your attention to look at your life and want to make some changes. It's helping open your mind to ask questions and seek answers. At some point along the journey, it's important to realize that the pain is a way to enroll you in to seeking a higher path, a path of awakening to your true self.

No matter where you are on that path, it is important to understand that until you pioneer and cleanse your emotional energy, you will carry a residue of sadness, anger, and other potent emotions. Those unresolved emotions are the fuel that feeds the creation of lack, pain, and struggle. Your emotional energy is one of the most powerful energetic forces in your life, both for creating what you don't want and creating what you do want. Overlooking this vital force in your quest for wellness will keep you from fully achieving affluence. We tend to focus a lot of our time on physical healing. Yet the emotional body has priority to the physical body. We might heal one physical issue, only to create another if we have not done the work of emotional healing.

Once you realize this, you begin to understand how important your feelings are. You will not be scared to feel your feelings and you actually invite the opportunity to feel what has long been overlooked and ignored. As you choose to fully feel, you start creating an entirely new emotional lifestyle—a lifestyle of emotional affluence.

Understand that, in order to feel the fullness of joy, you have to allow yourself the space to feel the opposite energy of emotional pain. In that choice lies your emotional freedom to live in the experience of the emotional now, feeling what your present life supports you in feeling, while being free of having to feel the painful feelings of your past.

Rather than thinking you're having to fix something, know that you're evolving, you're waking up, you're learning tools to create an affluent life. You're activating your soul's energy, your soul essence. And that becomes your new lifestyle, your new way of being. As you continue to do your emotional healing work, your life will look very different a month, six months, a year from now. I'm not the same person I was even a year ago or five years ago. I even look different. I just keep getting more emotionally clear and present. It's become a lifestyle for me to have permission to feel my feelings. I invite you to this lifestyle. It's a beautiful way to live, to get to a place emotionally where you feel emotions that reference your current reality instead of repressed or overly charged emotions from your past.

Emotional affluence is a state of joy. How often do you feel peace and joy for no apparent reason? As you go about your day, take note of the times when you're smiling. When did you have a pleasant feeling? A thought of appreciation? Where is the affluence showing up for you emotionally today? Look at your past week and note when you felt peace and joy or a state of inner happiness. How often did you feel it?

As we become more technologically advanced, it is vital that we also advance our humanity to become a kind, civil, and collaborative society instead of a competitive warring one.

Your Outer World

There are three areas of our outer world experiences that we will explore in this book: your physical body, your financial experience, and your relationships (primarily your relationship with a significant partner).

All outer world experiences are subject to the state of your inner world. The inner world creates the outer world. If your thoughts and feelings are full of lack, pain, and struggle, and you are disconnected from your spiritual authority, you will experience lack, pain, and struggle in all or some of your outer world creations. It is up to you.

Here's an interesting discovery: the more you create affluence in your inner world, the more you let go of the need for things and stuff in your outer world. As you raise the vibration of your inner world experience, you may want to simplify your outer world experience. This is a common experience. You want less, as you no longer attach your sense of value and worth—your inner self—to property owned and acquired in the outer world. You are no longer running after what you thought you wanted! You will experience what is correct showing up as you have now set the stage for affluence in your physical reality.

"When I run after what I think I want, my days are a furnace of distress and anxiety; If I sit in my own place of patience, what I need flows to me, without any pain. From this I understand that what I want also wants me, is looking for me and

attracting me. There is a great secret in this for anyone who can grasp it." —Rumi

Let's take a look at what affluence looks like in the outer world manifestations of our physical, financial and relationship experiences.

What is Physical Affluence?

The body is the vessel for the soul to experience this realm. When we are living in physical affluence, we love and honor our bodies. We show appreciation for our bodies by taking great care of our physical self.

Sometimes we treat our body as if it were a small child that needs to be shamed or punished. You may be treating your body now the way you were treated as a child. Do you believe that your body is not good enough? That it is flawed and dysfunctional? How do you speak to your body? Do you feel dissatisfied with its appearance, size, and functionality? As long as you view your body as inadequate and believe it needs to be "fixed," you'll be frustrated with it and not be able to access the affluence your body has to offer you.

The truth is, your body is a beautiful, intelligent part of you. It responds very well to respect, patience, love, kindness, and it has its own healing abilities. You have an amazing system of healing held within the body. Your body is an affluent system of natural healing, repair, and regenerative powers when given the chance to perform these powers. All bodies are amazing systems that are capable of physical affluence.

If your body was born with physical limitations, you are a great example of how the functional parts of your body can make up for other parts and systems of the body that do not wholly function. Only you know what your soul's experiences should be when it comes to your body's functionality. Some people's souls have chosen a lesson of physical disability as part of their experience in this lifetime. I have seen a repeating pattern that many people, especially children with disabling conditions or short lifespans, seem to have an understanding that they can experience a life of affluence, ease, and joy, despite any limits of their body. Even if their understanding is not conscious, on some level, their soul seems to embrace their experience with less judgment than others might expect. Of course, everyone responds differently to challenges, and this sense of understanding and acceptance isn't true in everyone's experience. But if you or a loved one experiences severe physical limitations, consider what your soul knows or their soul knows about this experience on a deeper level.

I don't know which life experiences your soul has signed up for. But I know you can get to a place of affluence with your physical body, which creates either a healing response or a perceptual shift in how you experience any physical disabilities. Too many of us have accepted unnecessary physical limitations as a part of life. In Part Two of this book, we'll cover the process of asking our soul what is correct for us and discerning the difference between what we want and what is correct.

As a function of our physical experience, we communicate. The words that we speak play a huge role in creating a life of affluence, ease, and joy. In Part Two, I dedicate an entire section to help you identify which words are keeping you stuck in lack, pain, and struggle, so you can change your word choice and language to ultimately change your life. What you think and feel turns into the words you put out into the physical world. Those words contribute to creating an abundance of whatever your current experience in life is. If you do not like what you are experiencing, change your words and your language.

Do you have a lot of pain and sickness? How's your energy? Are you vital and vigorous? Is your health thriving? Is your body regenerating and doing what it's designed to do because of its amazing intelligent system?" Let wellness, vitality, strength, and zest for life become your body's natural and familiar state."

What is Financial Affluence?

Think back to when you started to learn about the law of attraction or the laws of creation. Was a lack of money your motivation to learn how to create more of what you want? We can thank money (or a lack of it) for helping so many of us turn within to start opening our eyes to our inner world of intuition and insight.

That was the case for my husband and me in the mid 1990s. We had created tens of thousands of dollars of consumer debt which was mounting every month during a period of unemployment. We felt increasingly powerless to change that debt as it grew. It was scary and our lives were going financially downhill fast. Our relationship was suffering, our parenting was affected negatively, our day-to-day spirits were declining, and our contentious interactions were on a rise the longer this went on. When you have financial lack and debt, every area of your life is affected, as money is a day-to-day commodity that is necessary to live in our modern world.

From 1994 to 1996, we lived nearly a year and a half in this state of lack, pain, and struggle before we started to study the teachings of Abraham Hicks and Louise Hay, which started to open our inner eyes and gave us the insights that were the beginning of an entirely new lifestyle of pioneering and healing our inner world.

Think back in your story. See when and how a lack of money moved you to turn within and open your inner knowing. Take a moment and thank money for playing this role for you. If it is still playing this role, you will learn in Part Two of this book how to suspend that pattern and allow money to show up for you to support your new life of affluence, ease, and joy.

I define financial affluence as having as much or more than I need. When we have financial affluence, we always have an excess. We have more money coming in than going out. I teach that money is a tool, a resource to support your life. It does not create affluence; it supports you in creating it. Purchasing is an exchange of energy that brings you what you enjoy and need and want in this lifetime.

In the world of financial abundance courses or money system courses, a fallacy is taught that everyone can or should be a millionaire. Years ago, as I taught my first training in manifesting money, I realized that many of the students I attracted wanted to become millionaires. Most people don't have the energetic set points for flow and accumulation to support that amount.

A million dollars is not in their spiritual blueprint, nor is that amount of money necessary for them to experience a life of affluence, ease, and joy. If you have thought that you want to create millions of dollars, this book will help you see if that experience is truly in your spiritual blueprint. If it is not, you will be able to adapt your thinking and focus on what is correct for you to materialize in the form of money, so you can align your energy with creating that.

Financial affluence is not a cookie-cutter idea. It's not being a millionaire; it's about living richly in joy, ease, and affluence. You might think having a $120,000 annual income is affluent. More or less than that may feel affluent for you. Your experience with financial affluence is your personal experience. One person's affluence is not the same as another's. You may find that much less money and a life of minimalism is affluence for you. This book will help you answer the question: What is financial affluence in your particular life?

The insights and awarenesses you receive from this book will support you in activating your unique blueprint of affluence as your reality. Expect it to look different from others. What supports you in feeling ease and joy in your life cannot be the same as another. An abundance of money (in whatever amount abundance means for you personally) is a tool to help you create your unique experience.

What is Relationship Affluence?

Affluent relationships are harmonious, cooperative connections, with fabulous communication, where both parties feel supported and free to be themselves. You have a variety of relationships with different people in your life, and you have the opportunity to experience affluence with all of them. Because the partner relationship is so key to the experience of affluence, that's where this book will focus. You can generalize the lessons you learn to other relationships.

As the consciousness of the planet continues to shift, we are shifting from an energy of hierarchy in our relationships to one of partnership. In the energy of hierarchy, there is always a dominant and subordinate role within a relationship. Modern society's traditional cultural mores have had men playing the dominant role and women playing the subordinate role. As of the 1960s, that energy began to shift and topple the hierarchical energy to allow an even playing field of women and men becoming partners.

My husband and I were married in 1980, which was still in the early days of this cultural and energetic shift from hierarchy to partnership. We have both acknowledged that we were married in the energetic construct of hierarchy, where he was expected to lead the family as the patriarch and I was to submit to his guidance. It didn't take long for us to experience that our personal energy was not designed for this energetic construct.

Even though we both tried with our best efforts, it never felt right, and trying to play those roles would often blow up in our faces. Little by little, we gave ourselves permission to create a relationship of partnership, which took us years to come to.

We had no role models or energetic templates to draw from. Both of us came from households where the man was dominant and the woman was subordinate in the energetic setup. Now, over thirty-eight years later, we have successfully divorced the energy of hierarchy and we create a relationship of partnership, where the state of affluence can now live and thrive daily. We are the parents of five grown children. Our shift into the energy of partnership has supported our children in creating their relationships in this same energy of partnership from the very beginning.

Partnership allows both parties to be themselves and feel honored. No one has to exist to please the other and accommodate them so that one person is always in the lead. Both people in the relationship come together to lead their family as they counsel together about what is correct for all parties involved.

In an affluent relationship, both parties know how important communication is, and realize it is the foundation of a strong relationship. Good communication develops trust, and trust develops unity and strong bonds. Affluent relationships are not free from upsets or discord. In fact, they are allowed and worked through using effective communication skills.

There's a concept called, "My *I am* is your *I am*." This means that whatever I am saying or thinking about you, I am saying or thinking about me. If I criticize you, I am criticizing myself. If I appreciate you, I'm appreciating myself.

Every time you get upset, bothered, or triggered by your partner, you have an opportunity to look at yourself. If you are well into your experience of creating a life of affluence, ease, and joy, you will not tolerate shaming or abuse in your relationship and would most likely not create this for yourself. (To be clear, people who are abused do not cause their abuse. They are living out certain energetic patterns. Recognizing and consciously shifting those patterns can help someone who has been abused to take their power back.)

Beyond your intimate, familial relationships, you create a relationship with groups in society. Do you participate in any group energy or collective energy (through activities or organizations) that compromise you or keep you stuck in lack, pain, and struggle? Which of those activities are timely for you to give up? Which boundaries do you need to set so that you can start to feel your own spiritual energy and vibration of affluence? If you're in an energetic soup that involves other people's energy day to day—television, media, music, movies, books, social media—where do you get pulled out? Where does your energy take a hit? Where are you compromising? Make some choices to claim your energy back and care for it properly. Make it a priority. Make choices that support your energy coming alive, your life force being able to hold the higher vibration of your spirit energy.

What if my partner is not interested in making these changes?

Since the greater part of my following is women, I hear this question often. I believe it is a woman's role to lead her family in the spiritual awakening that is happening on our planet. Women are innately endowed with a nurturing energy, an energy of birthing. Whether you are a woman or a man reading this book: It is the feminine energy within all of us that is birthing a new reality of joy, affluence, and ease.

Trust that if your partner is not yet choosing to do his or her own inner work or is not making changes that allow the partnership to release patterns of lack, pain, and struggle, that does not mean you have to wait. Someone needs to lead out.

Women may tend to wait, to either be led by or assisted by their partners in many experiences in life. This comes from an old energetic pattern of the patriarchal energy leading the matriarchal energy—men leading women, with men in the energetically dominant role and women in the energetically submissive role. This patriarchal hierarchy is no longer required in our mortal experience. Part of the collapse of this former hierarchy is seen in women leading a spiritual awakening.

Women shift the energy of their partnership by moving forward in their own awakening. Women pave the way for their partners to come along the path as well.

Of course, you would like to talk about your newfound awareness and a-ha's with those you love most. That time will come. It's best to allow your partner to come to their own shift in their own time. You will be led to know what to say, when not to share, and most of all, when to not try to enroll your partner in the process. We all have our own soul timing and soul lessons of what is correct for us and when. Trust your process and trust the process for others in your life.

If you are looking for support and connection while going through this shift, I invite you to join a community with like-minded people. Community is important at the time in which we live. We used to have a built-in community experience with our families and neighborhoods. But several decades ago, the cultural community started to shift as we were all launched on different paths of finding our true selves. We can often feel alone as we navigate the inner space of our selves which can dramatically change the landscape of our outer experience. Being a part of a community of like-minded people helps us with that very personal process.

You may find that what you believe and aspire to looks and feels very different from any other member of your immediate family. Sure, you can talk about surface-level-experiences of your life, but the deeper, more investigative conversations are uncomfortable. I believe the internet provides us with the ability to connect with other like-minded people where we can mentor each other by sharing our stories, challenges, and successes. Use the internet and social media platforms to help fill your energy rather than deplete it.

I invite you to join the supportive online communities I host with my team (you can find more information in the appendix). You will find like-minded people who support each other in navigating the nuances of their daily experiences to create more affluence in every area of their lives.

My I am is your I am. Whatever I am saying or thinking about you, I am saying or thinking about me. If I criticize you, I am criticizing myself. If I appreciate you, I am appreciating myself.

Parent/Child Relationships

Although the relationship lesson in this book will focus mainly on partner relationships, I will share some notes on parent-child relationships. Alongside your relationship with a partner, these relationships have great capacity for either struggle or joy. You'll find guidance for raising affluent children in all six lessons. Whether your children are little or grown, you still have an influence in your children's lives to help them shift from patterns of lack to the patterns of affluence.

The two primary ways you can help the generations that follow you:

1. Clear your own generational patterns of lack and struggle and
2. Model to them what it looks and sounds like to live an affluent life.

Clearing Your Own Generational Patterns

As you clear and heal from your mental, emotional, and physical patterns of lack and struggle, you energetically and even biologically pass on the benefits of your own clearing to your posterity. You are a generational carrier of thought patterns, feeling states, and DNA inheritances that can stop with you. Fascinating research in today's science shows how the effects of emotional trauma can be carried across generations.[vii] The same is true for other emotional states. Even your grown children can benefit unknowingly from the way your healing efforts shift the energetic dynamics of your family.

71

As a parent, you are gifting your children, your grandchildren, and beyond the opportunity to be free of unnecessary lives of lack and struggle. Because of you, they can more fully manifest the richness of an affluent life from the very beginning of their lives.

Energetic Cultural Structures

Another energetic phenomenon that is occurring on the planet is a side effect of the rising Schumann resonance.[viii] Schumann resonances are electromagnetic waves in the atmosphere across the globe (named for a physicist who predicted they existed in the 1950s). The frequency of these resonances can rise and fall, but in the past, the overall frequency has remained fairly constant. In just the past few years, Schumann resonance frequencies have increased by five times. A shift like that in the earth's entire electromagnetic field has a huge impact on us! Energetic structures that have been practiced as social norms have kept humanity doing what has been perceived as acceptable and proper for the time period. Those energetic structures and overlays on the collective energy are being released and changing ever more rapidly.

Historically, you can look back and see shifts that have occurred in each decade. Consider what has been socially acceptable in each period of time. When the upcoming generations abandon those beliefs and social norms, the resulting difference between the older and younger has been referred to as the "generation gap." The gap is the space created when the next generation abandons the ways of the previous generation and there appears to be little connection between the groups and what they each perceive as "right and socially acceptable."

The truth is, your children are not born with the same energetic structures held in their personal energy system as you were. They are more energetically open. They have more open minds and open heart centers. In the Sanskrit system of chakras, these centers are referred to as the crown and heart chakra. These energy centers used to be heavily influenced by the energy of the collective consciousness. Children who were born since the turn of the 21st century are independent of that collective influence. They can think and feel more independently of the collective and the familial energetic systems they were born into. This is a great opportunity as parents to be role models and mentors to your children in learning how to create an affluent life.

Modeling Affluence to Your Children

As you model new patterns of affluence in your day-to-day life, you teach your children by example. The younger your children are, the more opportunity you have to influence how they perceive and interact with the world.

My children were in their grade school years when my husband and I began to model new patterns of living an affluent life. We started to change how we perceived the world, how we spoke about our circumstances, what was possible for us. We were both personally enrolled in healing our own generational patterns. We would talk about what we were learning with our children and teach them how they could apply these new principles and practices in their life. We taught them about generational patterns and how they could clear them, as well. At an early age, they began to learn that they had a choice of how to respond to what

73

materialized in their lives, to either suffer or celebrate what is, and also how to influence their day-to-day events to unfold in alignment with their soul purpose.

Certain generational beliefs are common among parents. For example, when it comes to financial affluence, many believe that you should go without in the early days of your adult life, or that struggle with insufficient money teaches you how to appreciate your life more. Too often, we tend to make money a moral consideration when it comes to how we perceive and speak about it with our children. I encourage you to separate your children's ability to be a civil, moral adult from how much or how little money they have. If you model for your children how to respect money as a tool, and to trust that they have an abundance of that tool at their disposal, you set them up to create financial gain earlier in their adult years. You may find that your good role modeling, paired with the benefit of being born with fewer energetic cultural overlays, allows them to become financially rich beyond what you have created. If their experience in financial affluence seems to surpass your own, I encourage you to notice if it brings up any old beliefs and perceptions up about them "needing" to go through financial hard times! Do any feelings of resentment or unfairness come up? If this happens, take time to clear these old generational patterns that are presenting for you.

You can also model affluence in your parenting when you know and understand your children's true natures, as I teach you in my best-selling parenting book, *The Child Whisperer*. When you understand your child's Energy Type (and your own), you are free to parent them from a place of honoring what motivates your child to develop and use their natural gifts successfully. You eliminate the need for shame-based discipline, and you allow and nurture open and honest communication with your child so they feel safe to share their best selves with you. It is a magical approach to parenting that will allow more affluence, ease and joy into your experience with your child. To learn more about *The Child Whisperer*, refer to the resource section of this book.

As I expect my every need to be met, it is.
As I expect clear answers to every challenge,
I am guided. As I expect affluence in
every area of my life, I receive it.

How Do You Know When You Are Experiencing Affluence?

Although the state of affluence is not your constant state, it is your natural state, your God-given creation that you are awakening in your being. As you clear away the old energy of lack, pain, and struggle, your state of affluence just comes to life. How do you recognize when that's happening? Here's a description.

At first, as you learn new skills and practice to make affluence a constant, it starts to become your new reality. You start to feel the condition of affluence as life is "getting better for you." Fewer struggles show up, more money flows in and accumulates, you experience more harmony in your relationships. To a degree, your inner happiness is still influenced by circumstances in your outer state. And then, something magical happens. You begin to feel the constant of peace, joy, and true happiness for no apparent reason! You start to experience moments of "all is well" as though you are suspended in pure happiness.

I remember one of the first times when this started happening for me several years ago. I was driving in the car one day and I started to feel happy without that feeling being attached to anything happening in my life. It was a state of happiness without any condition and without any connection to any particular event.

That's what you're striving for—to get in touch with the God-given energy of affluence that you naturally hold in your being. You might just sense it in periodic moments in the day, when for no apparent reason, you're feeling pleasant or happy. You might sense it and notice it when things just line up for you, as your daily experiences open up and fall into place.

In my journey of shifting from a reality of lack, pain, and struggle, to a reality of affluence, ease, and joy, I have found the process takes time and it is something that happens piece by piece. We can shift our energy and our beliefs instantly. But the practice of shifting our entire reality (and making it stick!) does not happen all in one day.

For me, as is true for so many others, the desire for greater affluence started in the financial realm. My husband and my state of increasing consumer debt painfully got our attention and became the catalyst to start to heal the inner world of our thoughts, feelings, and beliefs about lack. We soon graduated to our relationship and spent years shifting it from the energy of hierarchy to the energy of partnership. The last energetic frontier has been our physical bodies. As we moved through shifting our outer world experiences from lack, pain, and struggle, we were always healing and pioneering the inner-world experience of our minds and emotions.

As was true for us, we spent years trying to "fix" the outer world by purely focusing on the problems and issues. After years of this, we learned that purely focusing on the outer world, without making changes in the inner world of thoughts and feelings, was like moving furniture you don't like around a room. Everything appeared to be in a different place, but we still didn't like the outcome. In other words, the furniture was the problem and we just rearranged when and how it showed up, but it was all still coming from the energy of lack, pain, and struggle.

I refer to this phenomenon as the "Groundhog Day Effect" that is so beautifully taught in the movie *Groundhog Day*.[ix] It's like waking up to the same day, day after day after day. Your outer world will not change until you pioneer and heal the inner world of old generational programming and patterns of lack, pain, and struggle.

This process is one that takes time, and that is something we have plenty of. All that is required of you is to show up each day with the intention that you are going to keep the process going.

You'll remind yourself frequently, as you once again try to move the furniture around to fix a problem or issue presenting in your outer world experience, that you need to go within and change the subconscious and conscious mind's patterns of lack, pain, and struggle. You need to activate the truths in your personal blueprint to consciously create affluence, ease and joy. Each time you do this, your ability to live an affluent life gets stronger and more consistent.

You are an engineer and you are either accidentally engineering your life or consciously choosing to engineer your reality.

You Have a Choice

You are a creator. You are either consciously or accidentally creating your life. Regardless of your level of awareness as a creator, creating is a function that you are involved in every day.

The process of creation occurs on an energetic level. Theoretic scientific models suggest that at our most basic level, we are energy.[x] Quantum field theory predicts that space is not empty at the quantum level, but instead, that it is full of energy, and that we are all connected at an energetic level. The source of the material world is the energy from the quantum field organizing itself into particles that materialize in our physical world.

It is so easy in the field of physics, in the field of medicine, in the fields of archaeology, to dismiss data that doesn't meet the model you are trained to think with. —Dave Asprey

In Part Two of this book, I am not going to talk about quantum mechanics or the reasons why we can affect the morphogenetic field we exist in. Rather, I am going to teach you in practical, actionable terms how to become an engineer in hacking your own reality from one of mediocrity, lack, pain, suffering, conflict, repression, and any other form of struggle, to a reality of affluence, ease, and joy.

I can't prove that you can influence reality. It just makes sense, given what I have studied, what I have seen in my own life and thousands of others, and what scientific evidence is showing us in the field of quantum physics. Consciousness study shows us that each of us is like an antenna, tapping into a field of information. On a daily basis, you are interpreting the field around you through your perceptions. You send your response to those perceptions into the field and the field is sending your interpretation back to you. You are both receiving and transmitting information at a quantum energetic level.

Yes, you can influence this field of intelligence. What you get back depends on what you are sending in. Your thoughts, feelings, and perceptions of reality become habits. They prompt you on a daily basis to interact with your reality in a way that creates patterns. You can stay stuck in those habits for years, or even for your entire lifetime. Generations have preceded you, sending and receiving the same information, creating patterns that existed long before your lifetime. Paying attention to what we think and how we feel, what we are feeding the field during the day, even if we spend just five minutes every day connecting and finding our center, can have a dramatic, positive impact in our lives.

As we observe our reality, we affect our reality to become more of what we are observing it to be. If you are walking around all day, full of anger (even anger held subconsciously) and smiling, the energy of anger will prevail in affecting what is showing up for you—which is most likely more experiences that you are angry about. If you are walking around thinking poorly of yourself, or thinking poorly of others, the Universe is going to respond to you with that level of energy as well.

More than any other time in history, you have an opportunity and challenge to shift from the collective experience of lack and pain, to affluence, ease, and joy. It is my intent that you will make that choice and begin the practice of affluence to let it become your new lifestyle. By making this choice, and intending to practice it in some way every day, your life will not even be recognizable to you in five to ten years. The choice is simple: keep doing what you are doing and keep getting what you are getting. Or: practice what you learn in this book and you get what is aligned with the truth of who you are—an affluent life experience. Guaranteed. It's just up to you! Choose it. Practice it. Allow it. Manifest it.

If you can train yourself in the way you view reality, you will have an effect on it.

The Power of Intention

Once you have made the choice to create a life of affluence, ease, and joy, the next powerful step is to set an intention. Intention is a powerful tool that sets the energy in motion to start the creation process.

Intention is the process of using the mental field, mental energy, and the practice of thought to organize energy on your behalf, in order to support your highest good. Intention can be expressed in a declaration, such as, "I am now creating a life of affluence, ease, and joy."

When you wake up in the morning and get out of bed, as you are setting your feet on the ground, declare the following, "As I wake up I am showing up to create a life of affluence, ease, and joy." Doing this each morning sets the energy into motion for that day. Start playing with the energy of the day you are living right now to create the lifetime you want.

When I teach about how simple and powerful intentions are, certain questions often come up: what about people who experience tragic life events? Are they creating those events? If we believe that we create our lives, are we also saying that if we experience tragic life events, we're responsible for creating them?

I believe there are two reasons people have these experiences. First, yes, people subconsciously create their experiences, as they do not know they can create something different. They may be living out deeply rooted generational patterns, continuing a story they're not even aware of. We are constantly creating our lives energetically, even if we're not doing so consciously. And second, their soul chose to have that experience. Let me explain.

I teach an online course called The 30-Day Money Cure. It helps people shift what they are energetically creating in their financial experience, so of course, the question of tragic life events came up. In one session of that course, a student posed her question like this:

"I have been blessed with the ability to travel throughout the world since I was a teen. I have lived alongside those with very affluent and blessed lives and those with very little and much suffering. In light of my experiences, it is very hard for me to understand/accept the concept of the law of attraction/our personal vibration and that we create our experience.

I have recently been reading a lot about civil wars in Africa and the terrible circumstances the people have lived through— children forced into becoming soldiers, families running for their lives and never seeing one another again as militias destroy the villages. Also, thinking about all the refugees that are fleeing war-torn areas. Did millions of Syrians really attract having their children and families being killed by gases and bombs?

I can't seem to make sense of how all this works together. My lack of understanding of these bigger issues makes it difficult for me to deal with my own personal issues of struggle and lack."

A fellow student shared the following personal story and insights:

"My husband is from another country that has been affected by terrorist groups wreaking havoc in their country. He had family members die at their hands. He lived in a shack with dirt floors, wondering where their next meal would come from. His parents heard of the "law of attraction" and began to study and transform their lives. They attracted money and change. They ended up going from suffering to flourishing in just a few short years. [sic]

They tried to share with others what they were learning and applying, they tried to help, but most were just unwilling to see that things could be different. There is hope for people around the world, no matter their circumstances."

This reminds me of some wording Wayne Dyer used in *The Power of Intention.*[xi] During his life, he spoke globally about affluence and the law of attraction. Often people would ask how he could be so happy, so confident in this idea of intending and manifesting prosperity, while seemingly so worry-free about difficult circumstances and lack throughout the planet. He said it is IMPOSSIBLE to feel sad/hurt/lonely/bitter/angry/sick enough to make even ONE person feel or get better. So, he focused his time and energy on what does work: influencing positivity and kindness and goodness and affluence everywhere he could.

Wayne Dyer made a choice aligned with his own powerful intention. That intention started into motion an affluent life experience. He left a legacy of affluent insights and teachings that all of us can still benefit from.

Make the choice today, right now, to awaken and live the energy of affluence. As you wake and start your day, set the intention for that day that you are now living an affluent life.

In your life, how much are you settling for less? How much do you allow and experience affluence, ease, and joy? When you hear questions like these, your mind may immediately go to a current experience that feels like a struggle. Or you may be thinking, "Carol, I don't live in lack, pain, and struggle! My life is pretty good. It could be worse!" No matter which thought is going through your mind, you have this moment to create what you want to experience more of next.

It's time—time for you to connect more powerfully with your soul purpose, to learn the lessons you're meant to learn, to have the experiences you're meant to have, and to give service that you are uniquely qualified to offer. I've been through this process myself and I can tell you that a life of spiritual, mental, emotional, physical, financial, and relational affluence is worth the journey. I'll guide you through it. Turn the page. Let's practice!

PART TWO

Creating Affluence
The 6 Lessons

When you set a clear intention, and make a decision to create something different for yourself, amazing things start to happen. The energy begins to align itself to create and manifest very different outcomes in the physical world.

How to Use These 6 Lessons

The following six lessons will teach you how to create the primary experiences of your inner and outer world as experiences of affluence, ease, and joy. This part of the book is more hands-on. I recommend dedicating one week of learning and practicing affluence for each lesson.

Each lesson starts with the **TEACHINGS** of that lesson's focus of the week. After you read through the Teachings, you will participate in a 3-step process:

Step 1: **CLEAR** the old energy and life patterns that are keeping you stuck in lack, pain, and struggle.

Step 2: **ACTIVATE** the energy of awakening truths that hold the energy and vibration of affluence, ease, and joy.

Step 3: **PRACTICE** new life skills that ground this energy in a new life practice to manifest an ongoing experience of affluence, ease, and joy in your day-to-day reality.

Before we jump into Lesson 1, I'll help you understand these three steps so you can get the most out of each one.

The 3-Step Process: Clear, Activate, and Practice

Changing your limiting beliefs and patterns about lack, pain, and struggle is kind of like upgrading your software. It's simple, but it involves a process and you have to consciously agree to it to set it in motion. You won't just wake up one day and think, "A-ha! I've upgraded!" Your part is needed.

It's a simple process of cause and effect: change the energy you are offering to the world, and you change the world you are creating for yourself. The origin of your current struggles is your energy. That energy is then created into beliefs and perceptions, which flow into the language you use and into the way you respond to scenarios that show up for you. This continues until you alter it. In the new formula of cause and effect you will practice in this book, you consciously choose the energy you want to exist in. Then you match that higher vibration with language and behavior that support more of what allows your affluent life to show up in greater and greater measure over time.

The first step toward making a change to affluence is clearing the energy that you have inherited from generations of your family that were required to live in a condition of suffering and sacrifice. You are no longer required to suffer; it is really just a habit now! Think of this first step of clearing as deleting the old software in your belief system.

To delete that old software, you'll use a clearing script, which is a list of statements that you will read out loud to release your old beliefs. Each lesson includes a simple clearing script. Reading the script out loud and stating that you release the old beliefs is enough to let them go and shift your energy. It's quite simple to clear away the energy of outdated beliefs and perceptions that we still carry around. That is why I have provided only one clearing script in each lesson. You will find more clearing scripts in the appendix of this book, to help you shift your mindset around other specific challenges and limiting beliefs. Clearing is simple. The energy clears on your command. Though the energy clears in a moment, grounding and living in the new energy requires repetition. The next steps will support you in creating new habits of thinking, feeling and doing.

The second step of the process is to activate the energy that will support new beliefs that embody truth. You carry an energetic frequency that is birthing itself inside of you and you can consciously activate it. With the shift in the Schumann resonance of late, these energies are easily activated. We are actually being forced into a clearing and activation process, whether we are conscious of it or not. If you have not cleared away the older energy when these new energies are activated, old energy comes to the surface and pushes itself up and out, which feels incredibly uncomfortable in our bodies and can wreak havoc in our lives. Choosing to be conscious of this process and work with it takes the crazy off of it and allows a more balanced experience in the process of awakening to your true self.

As you are working with this internal shift of raising your vibration, it is important to enroll yourself and commit to the third step. Practice calls for daily commitment and repetition in choosing and practicing new skills in your day-to-day lifestyle. How you talk, what choices you make, your perception of your world, the thoughts that run through your mind, your behavior towards others—all are functions of your daily habits that have been running from a lower vibrational frequency. As that vibration rises, you have to change those habits to hold the new energy of your truth.

In today's world, we are often sold on lofty promises of how to create everything you want in 30 days! It has been my experience that changing the long-term side effects of generational patterns, both in our own lives and the lives of our posterity, is not an isolated 30-day event. You can certainly start there, but lasting change requires a commitment of showing up each day, making little changes, tweaking this and that along the way, and noticing both the big changes and the little signs that you are progressing. You may even move through phases of feeling like you are regressing or you're back where you started, only to realize that you are so committed that you are willing to go to the bottom of the barrel on old, repeating patterns so they are gone once and for all.

Life is a series of events that play out perfectly as you enroll yourself in the practice of the six lessons. Trust that you are being presented with scenarios perfectly designed for your learning and growth. At times, you may feel that the Universe does not have your back and that there is a conspiracy to take you out! I do believe you will only be given as much as you can handle, even when you are feeling enough is enough. The reward for sticking it out is great. By seeing it through, you are birthing yourself from a generational energy that has and is keeping humanity captive in a constant state of getting by and surviving.

What used to be considered *The Road Less Traveled* is now becoming the road more traveled—even if it is not yet the road mostly traveled.[xii] You are helping pave that road for generations to come.

How to Move Through the Lessons

I recommend you start with Lesson 1 and move sequentially through each lesson to Lesson 6. The order is intentional and you will get your best results by following it. Do one lesson and its corresponding practices for one week. Commit to do this for the six lessons, taking six consecutive weeks. You do not need to read through all six lessons before beginning.

After you complete your first six-week experience of going through all the lessons sequentially, you can decide which areas of your inner and outer world need the most attention and are calling for you to shift them. I recommend that you focus on the lesson that calls to you for as long as it feels supportive, then move to the next most supportive lesson. How do you know which lessons are calling to you? The answer is simple. Which areas of your life are presenting the most pain and struggle to you? Those are the ones that are asking for attention.

In the clearing section of each lesson, you will first identify where your biggest struggles are to bring the energy to the forefront. Once you bring the energy of old patterns to the forefront, you can easily clear them by reading aloud the clearing script I have provided.

Once you clear old energy, you create space to activate truth and allow that truth to permeate your being. You will do this with the activation scripts I have provided.

Then, you practice. After you have created a new energy to live in, you need to ground that energy into your body and day-to-day physical experience to create the reality you are designed for. Each lesson lists practice activities for the week that will help you ground the new experience of affluence that you want to create. You will have to get used to things going so well and a new normal of affluence, ease, and joy.

The lessons are simple. Make sure to not overlay your patterns of struggle on the lesson experience. There is a good chance you will, as that is what you are used to. Find ways to hold yourself accountable. (I recommend that you check into the additional resources I list in the back of this book. The online groups I host can help you stay accountable, as many students are willing to give loving feedback to help you see what you have blinders to.)

You are embarking on a six-week experience that can bring lasting affluence into your life, if you allow it. Although the life changes you experience may be large, the 6 Lessons are truly a line-upon-line journey each day. There is no perfect way to move through the lessons. There is only your way. Let's get started!

How to Create Spiritual Affluence

Teachings: Being Your Own Spiritual Authority

The energy of spiritual authority is shifting. For a long time, we have looked outside ourselves for direction from ecclesiastical leaders, religious authorities, and gurus, who tell us what to believe and how to connect with divinity. We are shifting from that experience to turning within to find that divine connection and those individual answers.

This doesn't mean we need to throw religion away or that it has no value anymore. It just means that you are the one in charge of your spiritual development, welfare, and knowing what is truth for you, rather than the person in charge being someone who plays the role of a religious leader in your life.

The people who play roles of religious leaders and influencers used to direct our spiritual experience. But that energy of direction has shifted to an energy of guidance, so the people filling those roles are guides for you now. Religion continues to offer a beautiful community experience for people to come together to worship, learn and practice the doctrines they hold as truth, give thanks and express their gratitude for the divine through prayer and song, and band together to make a difference in the world. Amongst the members in today's religious congregations, you will find more and more variety in how families and individuals of each congregation interpret and practice their religious beliefs within their developing spiritual experience of becoming their own spiritual authority.

You are in the process of becoming (or have already acquired the status of being) your own spiritual authority. It can be challenging in the early stages, as you may doubt and question your right to know what is correct solely for yourself when it comes to spiritual truths. You may not trust yourself or believe you have that right.

People have operated for a long time in collective pods that have been compliant to shared belief systems in cultural communities, families of origin, and marriages. We have long held the collective experience that we either need to be in compliance with the beliefs of all those who are part of our collective group or stay quiet. There has not been much opportunity to be nurtured to what individually supports us spiritually. Between the ages of 12-18, it's a natural process for all of us to find our own spiritual value system and start developing our spiritual compass to direct and guide our lives. Ideally, our parents would have supported that process. But few of us come from homes where our personal spiritual authority was nurtured by our parents. The good news is, you can set yourself up internally to allow more freedom for this part of you to continue to develop and grow.

The energy that influences your experience of being an individual amongst a collective energy—the energy of your root chakra—is shifting from the former belief of, "I need to give up my individualism in order to help the tribe survive," to, "I need to find my true individualism in order to help the tribe thrive." Whether you are consciously aware of it or not, you are being moved to that place of knowing and being your own spiritual authority. Knowing this allows you to trust the process and navigate this shift with more ease. Consider the possibility that you have been a part of a collective agreement with the souls of humanity to live at a time to help this shift occur.

Our extended family systems are evidence of this shift of people becoming their own spiritual authority. Look at your extended family. Notice the variety of experiences that your family members represent when it comes to what they believe and how they practice or honor those beliefs, especially their spiritual beliefs. Look back 100 years in your family history and you will not find this same level of variety and diversity. Families are learning how to stay united and close through other common associations and similarities, as it is rare that all family members experience their religious and spiritual beliefs and practices the same any more.

If you are a parent, you may have noticed that the children being born to you are more fully awake in their consciousness and exhibit a strong confidence in being their own spiritual authority. People like you have helped open this energetic environment to exist for the next group of souls to be beneficiaries of your inner work.

Many old beliefs and programs in our generational energy connect surviving and sacrifice to greater spirituality. In the next few pages, I'll share five common beliefs that people hold about their spirituality, either consciously or subconsciously. As you read, circle those you feel are still playing out for you. This will help bring to the surface which old beliefs and programs you are ready to clear. You can unhook your energy from to the need to suffer and sacrifice as part of qualifying as a spiritual person.

1. OLD BELIEF: I must deny pleasure. That is the spiritual path.

This generational belief was commonly practiced by our ancestors to show favor to God. Our ancestors' belief was, "In order to have goodwill in God's eyes, I must sacrifice and go without. That's the spiritual thing to do." Denying the pleasures of food, sexuality, good health, wellbeing, and amazing living spaces and environments is a practice strongly programmed into humanity. Notice when you're still being pulled in by the belief that you must deny pleasure because that is somehow a more spiritual path. Consider the possibility that you can connect with God while experiencing the blessings that life has to offer.

2. OLD BELIEF: It's more spiritual to go without.

In the field of energy psychology, this belief is referred to as a *psychological reversal*. This is a concept Donna Eden taught about in her energy medicine trainings. In a psychological reversal, you accept something as true when there's no truth to it, and you live it as though it were accurate. It's not true that it's more spiritual to go without, yet if you accept that as truth, you'll need to go without. Why? In your quest of living your spiritual truth, you'll subconsciously require yourself to go without in order to obtain something you value—your spiritual integrity.

This belief sets up a pattern that is constantly counterproductive. For example, you may want to increase your income, yet your value to be in spiritual integrity with God is a more powerful value to you than having more money. Which one will win out? The spiritual one will win out every time. As a result, you may feel as if you're getting ahead. In fact, you may even see more increase in your finances, only to have an unexpected expense or challenge that requires money to resolve it, which just keeps setting you back to the place of struggle with money.

So, what do you do? Clear the old belief and activate new beliefs that are aligned with true spiritual values. God created an ever-expanding Universe which you are naturally a part of. Growth and expansion is a natural law. Changing your beliefs will flip you from the belief of, "It is more spiritual to go without," to a belief of, "It is more spiritual to allow growth and expansion in all that blesses my life."

Consider the possibility that you may not be the author of this belief. Most likely, the origin of the energy driving this belief comes from your ancestors. Understand that going without may have been required for your ancestors, due to cultural standards, political climate, and laws of their time. It is no longer necessary in most parts of the world today. But if the energy of this story has never been cleared and the old programming has not been deleted from your personal energy system, it could still be holding you captive to living in unnecessary lack, pain, and struggle.

Many years ago, my husband experienced a pattern of never getting ahead with his career. He would make strides in creating more success, only to experience one setback after another. As we reviewed his family history, we found an event with his third great-grandfather. This grandfather was successful in his trade as a brick mason in a developing city in the mid-1800s. At the height of his career, he was asked to give up his lucrative business and lead a group of people to establish a new territory as they were seeking more religious freedom. This "call" came from a high-level ecclesiastical leader of the religious group he was a member of. He was basically asked to give up his career and business for the pursuit of more religious freedom for his family and community members. My husband's family had practically given this ancestor sainthood, as his choices were revered as holy. His story had been repeated through the generations as a model of how to be more spiritual.

As I assisted my husband in clearing this "energetic" family history pattern that was created years ago, he had a profound experience during the session of this ancestor coming to him and thanking him, as it was an energy that had never been cleared from the family story.

It's important to understand that during that ancestor's time-line of living, his choice was both correct and necessary to support what he wanted for his family and community. It is appropriate to share our ancestors' stories and express our gratitude for the choices they were required to make that bless our lives. Yet it's also important to recognize that times are different and those same choices of going without no longer represent our spiritual value. If you eulogize your family members and use their stories to reinforce that it is more spiritual to go without, you feed that energy and activate those patterns to have more life and power. Choose to share their stories in a way that expresses gratitude for what was necessary for your ancestors' time and believe that we can now be blessed with all that is good and also be spiritual people. Going without and spirituality are no longer connected in the time and cultures in which we live.

Review your family history to see if any family members in your generations of the past gave up their freedoms and comforts of life for religious reasons. What religious ties and affiliations did your family have? What was required of them to show God their faithfulness? Is the energy of this story still running in your life and your family's life? You may not know individual stories. How do you know what lies in your ancestral energetic imprints and patterns? Just look at your life and see what keeps manifesting and material-izing! That is all the evidence you need to know there is some old stuff hanging out in you! As you become aware, you can clear the energy of this family story, and the energy will start to clear.

Write a synopsis of the story here:

3. OLD BELIEF: Life needs to be hard in
order for me to grow spiritually.

Were you taught that you need some amount of struggle in your
life to be humble and appreciate what you *do* have? Do you have
a pattern of things getting better for you and then something
appears to sabotage that momentum? Are you put back in your
place and feel like you are being humbled? Consider if you use
expressions such as, "I always learn more when things are hard."

These are all signs that you have a deeper belief of, "Life
needs to be hard in order for me to grow spiritually." What would
it feel like to give up this belief? Do you trust yourself enough to
believe you could even be more spiritual if you were experiencing
affluence?

If you are a prayerful person, notice the wording of your prayers for clues about your status with this belief. Read the following phrases. If you use them in your prayers, you have positioned yourself in a place of lack and struggle to support you in turning to God for assistance:

- *"Please help me to overcome..."*
- *"Forgive me for..."*
- *"Give me the strength to..."*
- *"I am sorry for my..."*

Notice any phrases that put you in a downtrodden position. Do you believe God wants you to struggle so you will be more submissive to God's influence?

Would you be comfortable using phrases like the following in your prayers?

- *"I am grateful that I am now learning and growing in joy."*
- *"Thank you, God, for creating me to be such a magnificent being."*
- *"Thank you for filling me with self-trust so I follow my spiritual authority to do what is correct for me."*
- *"Thank you for all of my continued blessings of affluence."*
- *"Thank you for opening my mind to how I can serve with my gifts more fully."*
- *"Thank you for helping me notice what is not honoring my truth and for inspiring my motivation to make changes that honor me and you."*

As you take on the new belief, "My life is full of affluent thoughts, feelings, and experiences that support me in growing more spiritually," you will see the evidence of your potential as one of God's creations. Only you are blocking yourself from the potential God has created you for. God doesn't create broken, unworthy people. Only people can project that label and illusion on themselves and others. God always holds us in the highest esteem, which I am grateful for. I believe that God's grace and ability to hold that projection of truth on us empower us energetically to keep showing up to reveal that truth to ourselves.

4. OLD BELIEF: I am not worthy of an affluent life.

I cover this in more detail in Lesson 5, which focuses on creating financial affluence. In this lesson, I would like to invite you to no longer make the practical experiences of your spirituality a moral condition. The truth is, you were born worthy. There is no acquisition of worthiness; it is a constant. You may have beliefs that certain choices create or diminish your worthy state of being. If you subscribe to that religious belief, I encourage to see it a bit differently. What if your worthiness was a constant, something you could never make void? Rather than determining your worthiness, what if your choices were either activating or cancelling out your true potential?

Your day-to-day choices have a cause and effect. For example, let's say you are a mom who had a rough day and lost your temper multiple times at your children. That does not make you a "bad mom." That makes you a worthy mom who has made choices that diminished your potential to connect with your children that day. The cause-and-effect equation we live in does not determine whether we are worthy or not. It just determines what we attract more of.

Feeling guilty about your choices is appropriate to encourage you to make different choices. But feeling worthless (in other words, not being worthy) as a person, keeps you from feeling motivated to make different choices. When you buy into the belief that you are "not worthy," you are more likely to behave as if you have less power to make changes. When you hold the belief, "I am a worthy and powerful individual who knows better and I'm committed to making the changes necessary that reflect the truth of who I am," you are more likely to make changes that support an affluent life materializing for you.

Rather than equate your state of worthiness with the effect of your less moral choices, see those choices as affecting the flow of what can show up to support you. The cause and effect of your choices is more connected to the energy you put out into the world, rather than your worthiness quotient as a human being. You are worthy, always have been and always will be.

5. OLD BELIEF: Authority figures always let me down.

This belief can lead to unnecessary suffering. The people who play the roles of religious leaders are just people. They may be faithful people with good hearts, but just like you, they run their own generational patterns and have their own wounding to heal. If you rely on their direction without checking into your own personal spiritual guidance system, you can find yourself in a place of disappointment.

For example, a former client of mine came to me to find help with her adult daughter who was married and raising a young family. She was conflicted with her daughter's decision to leave the religious practice she was raised to believe was correct and true. This was an earth-shattering decision to my client. I asked her what she was the most scared of. She responded: "I just don't want my grandchildren being raised without the influence of God in their lives." That was a fair and reasonable concern. It seemed motivated by the correct desires for her posterity, rather than fear of what others thought, needing to keep up appearances, or equating her daughter's spirituality with her religious practice. That's an important distinction.

As we explored together further, we discovered possible reasons for her daughter's sudden and dramatic change of mind in what she believed. We traced back a pattern that started in her childhood. My client had an unfortunate and "ugly" divorce when this daughter was in grade school. The daughter had suddenly been let down by both Mom and Dad and began to not trust authority figures. At this time, she turned to religion to replace her mom and dad as her new authority figures. She became immersed and involved in her religion's practices, making sure she did everything right so she could please God and be blessed. With that same pattern having an energetic hold on her subconscious mind, it was only a matter of time until the next authority figure would let her down and she had to leave her religious practice in order to stay true to herself and the pattern.

Which decisions around your religious or spiritual practice have been influenced by hidden beliefs originating in your childhood or in your ancestors' stories? Which of those beliefs keep you from making the most clear and honest decisions that are truly for your highest good?

As long as we have hidden beliefs, we have hidden energy patterns that support old stories getting re-created over and over. The story may have different players and different surroundings, but the same struggle keeps us from truly being our own spiritual authority, with a loving God helping to guide our lives through the power of grace and joy.

Reflecting on Your Soul Purpose

Earlier in this book, I taught that your soul chose to have a mortal experience for three main reasons: lessons to learn, experiences to have, and service to give. Ponder on your life experience for the past five years and note what your experience has been in these three areas.

Lessons to Learn

Does it appear that your lessons are still the lessons of surviving or going without? Or have you graduated to the lessons of living in joy and affluence? Which lessons do you believe you came here to experience?

Circle how you would finish this sentence: Based on my experience of the last five years, my lessons could be categorized as...

A. *Lack, pain, and struggle lessons.*
B. *Affluence, ease, and joy lessons.*
C. *Some of both.*

Remember, you are no longer required to learn the lessons of lack, pain, and struggle. Continuing to do so is a habit. You are ready to graduate to the lessons of affluence, ease, and joy. It just takes awareness, clearing out the old, and practicing the new!

Write your lessons of lack, pain and struggle over the last five years:

Write your lessons of affluence, ease, and joy over the last five years:

Experiences to Have

Again, looking at the last five years, can you say you are having the experiences that bring joy to your heart and vitality to your soul? What would you like to do and experience more of in your life? Do you believe it is truly possible, or just a pipe dream that you can only consider but never realize?

Your soul came here to experience this world—the lands, the cultures, the flavors, the sights, the learning, the understanding and growth that can so readily be obtained at the time in which we live. If the experiences you truly desire are not materializing in your world, is the main reason your old belief in having to live a life of lack, pain, and struggle?

Note the experiences in the last five years that have brought joy to your heart and vitality to your soul:

List 10 things you would like to experience in the next five years:

1.

2.

3.

4.

5.

6.

7.

8.

9.

10.

Service to Give

We are all born with natural gifts and talents that we are meant to use to serve others. We often limit our definition of service to time or money given to a non-profit organization or to people in need. We can expand that definition. Every day, you come across people who are in need—in need of your smile, in need of a word of encouragement, in need of a helping hand, in need of just being respected and appreciated.

We are also meant to use our gifts and talents to serve others in a bigger way. More and more people are aligning with opportunities to use their gifts in the service of others. More and more, people's occupations are aligned with their gifts so that every day becomes an act of service. I know this is true for me. How are you contributing to the betterment of humankind on a daily basis? It doesn't have to be grand. It can be small, as small adds up to substantial over time. As you allow yourself to experience more affluence, ease, and joy in all areas of your life, you naturally have more time and more money at your disposal to support you in serving more. Allow this to happen and choose to be the spiritually affluent person you were born to be.

List five ways in which you are currently serving in the world.

1.

2.

3.

4.

5.

List three ways you are feeling called to serve that you currently do not. Write any perceived limitations that cause you to believe you cannot serve in the way you feel called:

1.

2.

3.

I say *perceived* limitations, as they are just that. You might say, "No, they are my reality." As you continue to believe that reality, it will be the reality you have to accept. Change your mind, change your reality.

Tips for Raising Spiritually Affluent Children

Children are being born today with their spiritual authority centers intact and fully functioning. The energy of humanity has been shifting away from spiritual power being outside of us to spiritual power being within us. Children being born now are arriving with that energy activated.

More than any other generation, millennials are choosing their religious and spiritual paths differently from their ancestors. They are deciding whether or not they want to follow a religious construct and leaders, and yet they are highly drawn to the spiritual and esoteric experiences that support them in becoming more self-realized. I shared a story earlier about a young man who chose to no longer participate in his family's religious affiliation. The experience in that story is happening increasingly, more than any other time in modern history.

Some may judge this choice of finding your own path as self-centered or apathetic. Yet, when you understand the difference in the design of this generation's personal energy system, you can see why they look within themselves to find answers, rather than looking outside of themselves to be told what to do.

When a child has the sense of being their own spiritual authority, and they are told they need to look for that power outside of themselves, they are more apt to pull away from that religion.

They feel a deep inner conflict within themselves. They can only know themselves as the authority over their spiritual experience and any resource outside of them is just a guide and support.

Knowing this can help you guide and support your children as they mature, to find their way within a religious construct or not, and to focus on helping them develop their spiritual authority center to help guide their lives.

The more pressure they feel that they have to believe and live a certain way to be accepted, the more they will pull away. Be a guide to your children and teach them how to practice their faith and spirituality in a way that honors their spiritual authority energy system that is already intact.

All of humanity desires to be part of communities that support us in doing good and making a difference. More and more, we are no longer looking to religion as a means to tell us how to live, but rather to guide us in making choices that align with religious or spiritual beliefs that we are empowered by.

Spiritual Affluence Step 1: CLEAR

Repeat the following clearing script out loud to clear and release your old spiritual beliefs and patterns of lack, pain, and struggle:

Remove from my conscious and subconscious mind an infinite number of lack and struggle beliefs and programs, including:

- *I think I need to suffer, struggle, and go without.*
- *I believe I need to suffer, struggle, and go without.*
- *I have to suffer, struggle, and go without.*
- *I really must suffer, struggle, and go without.*
- *I want to suffer, struggle, and go without.*
- *I deserve to suffer, struggle, and go without.*
- *I know I have to suffer, struggle, and go without.*

Remove and erase any and all energetic imprints in my spiritual, mental, emotional, and physical energy bodies that I inherited from my family that have contributed to or created suffering and struggle in my life story.

Release all beliefs and programs that have attached suffering and sacrifice to bringing me closer to God.

Release any inherited programs from my ancestors' stories that suggest suffering and sacrifice are necessary to do God's will.

Release any and all beliefs and programs that keep me creating patterns of lack, including:

- *I must deny pleasure because that's the spiritual path.*
- *It's more spiritual to go without.*
- *Life needs to be hard in order for me to grow spiritually.*
- *I release these beliefs, programs, and patterns with grace and ease.*

Spiritual Affluence Step 2: ACTIVATE

Repeat the following activation script out loud to help you start creating spiritual patterns of affluence, ease, and joy:

I am now free to create a life of affluence, ease, and joy. I activate in my conscious and subconscious mind the energy, beliefs, and programs of affluence, ease, and joy, including:

- *I think of a life of affluence, ease, and joy.*
- *I believe in a life of affluence, ease, and joy.*
- *I am ready to receive a life of affluence, ease, and joy.*
- *I want a life of affluence, ease, and joy.*
- *I deserve a life of affluence, ease, and joy.*

I know I am ready to practice the life skills that support me in creating a life of affluence, ease, and joy.

I activate and energize my spiritual, mental, emotional, and physical bodies with affluence, ease, and joy.

I now choose to be my own spiritual authority and to take ownership of my spiritual experience. I am guided by the Divine in knowing who to look to in order to guide me on my spiritual path.

It is spiritual to experience an abundance of that which brings me joy and pleasure.

It is spiritual to receive and to give. I allow great things to show up in my life so I can give more.

Life is full of affluence, joy, and ease, and I continue to grow spiritually.

Spiritual Affluence Step 3: PRACTICE

For one week, do the following activities to help you ground the new energy of being your own spiritual authority into your life practice.

1. Your mantra for this lesson is: *I wake up, I get up, I show up. I am doing what is correct for me today.* Using a dry erase marker, write this mantra on your bathroom mirror and repeat it every morning.
2. Read or listen to the Clear and Activate scripts for spiritual affluence each day.
3. Every day this week, spend five minutes in a quiet place, just with yourself, free of any noise or distractions. Turn your attention inward and just listen. If your mind begins to wander, turn your attention to your breathing to quiet the mind so you can be present in the solitude of your inner world. This practice will start to open your inner eyes and insight.
4. Journaling exercise. Answer and reflect on your answers to the following questions this week:

A. I feel my connection to God most often when I am...

B. Three examples of when or where I feel like I am my own spiritual authority:

C. I notice that I give my power away and do not feel like
my own spiritual authority when:

5. Each day this week, notice the moments when you give
your spiritual power away to others. When do you ask
for permission to do what you want? Who brings up
your impulse to justify, defend, and explain yourself?
Every time you feel the need to justify, defend, or explain
choices that you feel are correct, you are giving your
power away. It is important to have daily awareness of
any habits of giving your power away to an authority
outside of yourself. As you change these daily habits to
becoming your own spiritual authority, you ignite in you
the power of creating a life of affluence, ease, and joy.
Track your experience here:

Day 1 of Lesson 1

Today I gave my power away by:

Once I noticed it, I made this change:

Day 2 of Lesson 1

Today I gave my power away by:

Once I noticed it, I made this change:

Day 3 of Lesson 1

Today I gave my power away by:

Once I noticed it, I made this change:

Day 4 of Lesson 1

Today I gave my power away by:

Once I noticed it, I made this change:

Day 5 of Lesson 1

Today I gave my power away by:

Once I noticed it, I made this change:

Day 6 of Lesson 1

Today I gave my power away by:

Once I noticed it, I made this change:

Day 7 of Lesson 1

Today I gave my power away by:

Once I noticed it, I made this change:

6. For additional support this week please use any of the Spiritual Clearing Scripts found in the appendix.

Insights from Lesson 1

Training your mind to be an affluent mind is where an affluent life begins.

LESSON 2

How to Create Mental Affluence

Teachings: Affirmative Thoughts & Affluent Language

Affluence starts with your thoughts. In order to create an affluent mind, you have to train yourself to have one. The simplistic analogy that has been said for decades is to "see the glass half full." This can be challenging for some, as they do not want to be in denial about reality. The trick is to deal with what reality currently offers you, and teach your mind to respond with confidence that you can bend the energy to change reality, by first altering your thought process to be a more affirmative one.

If you really listen to your thoughts, you may be surprised by how often you cast yourself in the role of a victim, as someone who things just happen to. We learn to think with a victim mindset in our families of origin, by listening to what our family members speak about. When I started to rehabilitate myself from living as a victim, one of the first things I did was to start training my mind to respond differently in thought and perception from how a victim would think and perceive. That process required me to pay attention to the words I used, both in my thoughts and in my speech.

How was your family's conversation, their talk, the words they used about their experiences in life? Did you live in mediocrity? Did you go without? Was that considered a good thing? Was it more valuable to suffer? Did you frequently hear any of the following statements? Circle any that you heard as a child:

Life is hard.

You have to struggle to get ahead.

There is never enough time.

We just have to learn to get by.

Don't expect the best.

Once-in-a-lifetime opportunity.

Get used to going without.

Can't get any better than that.

I would rather die than keep on dealing with this.

I can't stand it anymore.

Why does this keep happening to me?

It's too good to be true.

Things never work out for me.

Don't expect it to last.

No pain, no gain.

It probably won't happen again.

I am always down on my luck.

If something bad is going to happen, it's going to happen to me.

Now underline any of the statements above that you say now.
How many of them are the same?

List any other limiting beliefs that were expressed in your family on a regular basis:

We develop our perception of the world as a struggle or a supportive, pleasurable place when we are young children. It has been common to believe that parents should teach children that life is a hard struggle and you shouldn't expect to get what you want. As young children, many of us were taught to think that way, both consciously and unconsciously. As teens, with an emotional need to "fit in," we continued the habit of thinking the way we were taught. As adults, we continue the thinking and speaking tendencies that express lack, because we haven't taken the time and dedicated the practice to changing. It seems that everybody thinks and speaks that way, and so we don't notice that anything needs to change. Again, I believe this lack-minded perception comes from old programming that we have a chance to wake up from at this time.

Having practiced affluent thoughts and speech now for over 25 years, I am aware of the theme of struggle that is woven into most people's thoughts and language. It's a habit. This habit of your inner world creates powerful daily interference that keeps you from bringing forth lasting positive changes in your outer world of health, relationships, and the amount of money you can flow and accumulate.

Think of a recent conversation you had with a friend or loved one. How much of your conversation was focused on how great life is going and how many good things you are expecting to show up for you? Most likely, the focus of the conversation was on what was not going well, what you are struggling with, and how hard life can be. You might think I am suggesting you just be a "Pollyanna" and pretend everything is great! Well, I sort of am, but there is a trick to this. It is not about being in denial and pretending everything is rosy in your life, which only causes you to disconnect from dealing with "what is" your current life. The trick is being fully aware and awake to what your life is right now, appreciating it, focusing on the good in it (as there is probably more good than not), and thinking and speaking affirmatively to throw more high-vibration energy at your life. What you think, you speak, and what you speak, you flow energy to in your life. It's a simple formula. Do you want to keep flowing energy to what you don't want? Or flowing energy to create more of what you do want? It is important during the practice of this lesson to be diligent in changing your thoughts and the words that follow them. How common is it for you to speak the language of struggle? Start paying attention to that every day this week.

Affirmative Self-Talk

One of the most common practices we use our thinking minds for is negative self-talk. In other words, we put ourselves down in order to maintain a negative opinion about ourselves. This practice is internal, but it also becomes outwardly evident if someone is berating others instead of themselves, as they have just taken their negative self-opinion and projected it onto to others. It is important to catch yourself in the practice of negative self-talk or negative references to others. Negative talk will keep you from living a life of affluence, ease, and joy, as this practice will alter your vibration so powerfully on a daily basis that you will never get any momentum in holding a higher energy.

At first, when you practice positive self-talk, it will not feel accurate to you. You will feel you are faking it. But you can "fake it 'til you make it." This is not new to you. This is old school Power of Positive Thinking 101. The difference in how you will practice it now, though, as part of a holistic, six-week practice, will train you to shift your energy once and for all. Changing your negative self-talk to positive self-talk is an important part of the full six-week practice of this book. A big payoff will start showing up in your life for the better as you no longer cancel it out by daily, low-vibration habits, such as negative self-talk.

Over and over, we can see that the most successful people—those who have acquired financial affluence and have influenced the world in a positive way—have trained their thinking minds to think positively about themselves and others. It's time for you to commit to do that as well, as you are meant to be affluent in your own way and free yourself up to make a difference in the world by serving with your gifts.

Ending the Self-Sabotage Game

We all have blind spots and strong conditioners that keep us believing and thinking the same thing over and over. These blind spots and conditioned beliefs create patterns of self-sabotage. We all want something better, yet we seem to settle too often and too easily.

The biggest player in creating self-sabotage patterns and tendencies is the function I referred to earlier: a psychological reversal. Let's explore it a little more. A psychological reversal is a deeper belief you still hold that gave you reason to create the original self-sabotage pattern. For example, imagine you are trying to drop some weight. Why is it that when you enroll yourself in new eating patterns, all you can think about is the food you are giving up and the freedom you believed you once had? Why does your mind hijack your efforts by obsessing about what you really don't want? It's a psychological reversal at play. There is a deeper belief operating in your subconscious that still believes you need the extra weight. Maybe you didn't feel safe in the world and extra weight creates a sense of a barrier or protection. Maybe you experienced sexual abuse and having an attractive body feels threatening. Whatever the deeper belief is, until you release and re-pattern that belief, it will set you up to sabotage yourself, as it has more power to win out than you think.

A client of mine was facing some important life decisions. She had a previous pattern of sabotaging herself that kept her from manifesting more of what represented affluence and joy. Because she felt afraid she would play out the same old sabotage patterns in the life-changing decisions in front of her, she had a hard time moving forward. Her psychological reversal, or what her subconscious said about this situation was, "I need to prevent sabotaging these decisions, so I just won't make them." I shared with her that awareness is the first step in shifting patterns of sabotage. I invited her to set this intention: "I am seeing my blind spots and becoming aware of my reversed thinking. As I do that, I free myself up to move forward successfully." I also invited her to ask her spiritual support team to prompt her and make her aware when she was about to play out an old sabotage pattern that she had become conditioned to. Once she knew the deeper motive for trying to "prevent sabotage," she realized she could move forward if she focused on creating what she wanted to experience, rather than trying to prevent something she wanted to avoid.

The clearing scripts in the appendix will help you clean up your subconscious and conscious mental field to help you free yourself from the self-sabotage game. It's worth the extra effort, as you will experience more success on an ongoing basis.

Prevention vs. Creation Thinking

Most people try to get what they want in life by attempting to prevent what they don't want! For example, you may try to prevent being late, gaining weight, aging, hurting someone's feelings, or causing an argument. Prevention thinking has an honorable motive. You try to prevent what you don't want, in hopes of getting your desired outcome: being on time, staying fit and healthy, taking care of your appearance, honoring others' feelings, or experiencing harmony in your relationship. The problem with the prevention approach to life is it causes a conflicting energy that actually stifles what you really want from showing up. What you focus on, you expand and create more of. Whatever you target with your thinking mind is energized.

Training your mind to switch from prevention thinking to creation thinking will allow you to more readily create your true desired outcome.

Use this simple three-step process to train your mind to focus on what you want, rather than what you don't want.

1. Think of something you are trying to prevent. Fill in the blanks: "I need to prevent _____ because what I really want is _____ . For example, "I need to prevent being late because what I really want is to be on time."

2. Now focus on what you really want and put your attention on it by saying, "I am choosing to create _____." For example, "I am choosing to create being on time."

3. Take a moment and imagine your desired outcome materializing. When that outcome happens, how will you feel and what will you say to yourself?

Tips for Raising Mentally Affluent Children

We develop how we perceive the world, what we believe, and how we speak about our beliefs in our families of origin.

Back in the years when our children were in grade school, my husband and I recognized that we could either set up our children to struggle and survive this world, as we had learned to do, or we could teach them how to be powerful creators who could thrive and still be humble, gracious people who chose to serve God and willingly share their gifts with others. During those years, I started to dramatically change my language. My husband and I made a conscious choice to teach our children the principles of choice and accountability and that they were creators of their lives. We began to tutor them in everyday scenarios, teaching them that their beliefs, thoughts, and language had a powerful impact on what they were experiencing. Because we started when they were so young, they didn't know that this was not a common practice. Sure, they spent time in their friends' homes, yet they didn't live with them to fully immerse themselves in the family cultures of their friends. Not until my daughter, Anne, went to college and lived full time with roommates did she discover that not everyone saw and spoke of the world in the way she had been taught—to know she had a choice to create something different, to know she was not a powerless victim to her circumstances. She was alarmed at how many negative references she heard and the self-defeating beliefs held by so many that life was hard and you just had to get by. She realized the gift she had been given by being part of a family household that taught her how to create a life of affluence, ease, and joy.

I suggest you continue going through the lessons in this book for yourself first, make some of your own changes, and then involve your children by example first, rather than by sharing. Be mindful to not require your children to learn what you are learning. If they feel pressured to do it, they will have less interest and will judge what you are doing as your next new thing! Give it time and make it easy by waiting for moments and opportunities to arrive for you to lead and guide your children in practicing affirmative thinking and affluent language. Again, example is the greatest tool you can use as a guide and teacher in your children's lives. Pray for your children to be open to your guiding influence, to want to learn what you are learning, and to practice what you are practicing. You will know when you achieve success with this because your children will start to correct your limited perceptions and lack-minded speech. Invite that correction and tell yourself you are doing a great job as a parent!

Mental Affluence Step 1: CLEAR

Repeat the following clearing script out loud to clear and release your old mental patterns of lack, pain, and struggle:

I now choose to release and let go of the patterns of limiting beliefs and thoughts.

I release these generational patterns as far back as they go, once and for all.

I release the habit of speaking the language of struggle and the need to put myself or others down.

I am free from the patterns of mental lack and limitation as they present in my thoughts and language.

It is done, it is done, it is done.

Mental Affluence Step 2: ACTIVATE

Repeat the following activation script out loud to help you start creating mental patterns of affluence, ease, and joy:

I now choose to activate my higher mind, my more conscious self to guide and assist me in creating new habits of thought and language that reflect the truth of who I am and who God created me to be.

I am now starting the practice of an affluent mind and affirmative speech.

Every day this week, I am super conscious of what I am thinking and what I am speaking.

When I notice the thoughts of lack and when I speak in limitation, I am catching myself and changing to thoughts of affirmation and words of affluence.

I am patient with myself as I notice old habits and change them.

As I commit to do this over the course of the rest of my life, I can only expect to create a life of affluence, ease, and joy.

I am committed and I am starting now.

Mental Affluence Step 3: PRACTICE

For one week, do the following activities to help you create a more affirmative mind and more affluent speech in your everyday life.

1. Your mantra for this lesson is: *I am grateful for my affirmative mind and affluent language.* Using a dry erase marker, write this mantra on your bathroom mirror and repeat it every morning.

2. Read the Clear and Activate scripts for mental affluence each day in the morning.

3. From the list below, circle the statement that most closely represents the phrases of lack you often express. Make note of the affluent phrase to use to replace it.

PHRASES OF LACK	PHRASES OF MENTAL AFFLUENCE
You have to struggle to get ahead.	I allow good things to show up in my life. I am always getting ahead!
There is never enough time.	What is correct for me shows up at the right time.
I can't stand it anymore.	This feels challenging, but since it's in my life, I know I can succeed.

PHRASES OF LACK	PHRASES OF MENTAL AFFLUENCE
We just have to learn to get by.	We get to learn to be open to allow affluence, ease, and joy.
I would rather die than have to keep on living with this.	I am concerned about that, and believe the correct outcome will occur.
It's too good to be true.	That's so good, it is true.
Don't expect the best.	I am learning to expect and receive the best for me.
If something bad is going to happen, it's going to happen to me.	It's amazing how many great things keep showing up in my life.
Can't get any better than that.	It just keeps getting better and better.
Don't expect it to last.	I am expecting it to only get better and to last.
Why does this keep happening to me?	This is so great, I am excited to see what else can show up.
I'm always down on my luck.	I'm grateful I'm so lucky.
Life is so hard.	Life is so amazing.

PHRASES OF LACK	PHRASES OF MENTAL AFFLUENCE
Get used to going without.	I am getting used to receiving more.
If something is worth it, it's worth sacrificing for.	If something is right, I am allowing it to show up in my life.
No pain, no gain.	I am open and accumulating all that is good.
Things never work out for me.	If it is correct for me, it always works out.
It probably won't happen again, it's too good to be true.	It just keeps getting better and happening again and again.
Once in a lifetime opportunity.	There are so many wonderful opportunities showing up in my life.

4. Every time you become aware that you are practicing limiting thoughts and speech patterns, stop yourself, change your thoughts, and change the phrase. This is key in shifting your energy from one of lack and limitation to one of affluence, ease, and joy.

5. Since it would be easy to just do what you usually do each day and forget to do #4, I recommend you set a reminder for every two hours on your phone, computer, watch, clock, or other device. When the reminder goes off, take a moment and reflect how the last two hours of

your day went. This may seem tedious, but there are big rewards for making these kinds of changes in your life.

6. Journaling exercise. At the end of the week, write some thoughts in reference to the following questions.

What have you noticed about your habits and tendencies with thinking and speaking limiting thoughts?

Do you think or speak in negative terms around certain subjects? Which ones?

Do you tend to think and speak in terms of lack at certain times of day?

Do you think or speak in terms of lack more often around certain people? Who are they?

Are you more vulnerable to thinking and speaking from a place of lack when you are tired or hungry? Write an example.

How successful were you this week in changing your thoughts and language to reflect the energy of affluence, ease, and joy?

7. For additional support this week, please use any of the Mental Clearing Scripts found in the appendix.

Insights from Lesson 2

Rather than choosing between a perspective of a glass half empty or half full, switch to this perspective: I am choosing to fill the glass!

How to Create Emotional Affluence

Teachings: An Inner Foundation of Peace & Well-Being

Your emotional body is the place where you feel your feelings. This area of expression has only been given attention by mankind in the last several decades. Look back to your own childhood and consider how much you believe your feelings were honored as a child. Were you encouraged by adults to feel your feelings, to express openly how you were feeling, or to put words to how you were feeling?

For most of us, the answer to those three questions is *no*. We were afraid to feel and express our feelings. More often than not, expressing our feelings got us into trouble.

We may have heard shameful feedback, such as:

- *I'll give you something to cry about.*
- *Stop whining and crying.*
- *I am going to leave you here if you don't stop.*
- *Stop being such a drama queen.*
- *What are you fussing about?*
- *Big girls/boys don't cry.*

During my private practice days, I heard the most horrendous stories about what parents would say to shame their children in order to get them to stop crying. Even though I had my own horrendous stories of mean things said to me by my father, I was still continually shocked to hear what some parents would resort to. Read the following examples to see what I mean. If you relate to any of them, I am truly sorry you ever had to hear any of these abusive phrases:

- *You'll be ugly forever and no one will ever love you if you don't stop crying.*
- *Go play in traffic.*
- *Those are "crocodile tears." (In other words, your tears and emotions are not real, and therefore, not valid.)*
- *Get out of my sight, you make me sick.*
- *I'll beat the sh** out of you if you don't stop crying.*
- *You're just crying to manipulate me.*
- *Out there in the real world, people don't cry when they get upset. You'll never make it out there.*

Some people were not allowed to show any emotion around actual physical pain. For example, a client of mine shared the following with me:

"Right before my junior year in high school, I walked around on a badly sprained ankle for a week because I didn't want to say it hurt. I had to learn how to act like my walk was normal, even though it was excruciatingly painful to put any weight on that

leg. My mom noticed that the Velcro on my Reeboks were uneven and that my left ankle was extremely swollen compared to my right. She freaked out and took me for x-rays. The doc said that the ankle was just this side of being broken and I needed to be in a splint for two weeks and walk on crutches. My dad asked me every day how long I had to be on crutches and wouldn't let me take any pain meds (because HE never did). As soon as my two weeks were up, I wasn't allowed to even mention my ankle. It should be fully healed, right?"

For many of us, expressing our feelings in childhood was often referred to as "throwing a tantrum." It made our parents uncomfortable and often triggered repressed emotions from their own childhoods, which they would then unleash on us. Fathers had more of a tendency to get angry with us and mothers either showed anger or played the martyr by telling us that our behavior made them feel sad. You might have thought that it was your job to keep your parents from either getting angry or feeling sad.

In my family of origin, our number one focus as children was to avoid doing or saying anything that could upset my father. Next to that, the unspoken assignment was to keep my mom from getting sad and depressed. Do you recognize similar roles you played as a child that put your parents' priorities ahead of getting in touch with your own feelings and learning how to manage and express them in a healthy way?

You may be one of the few in your family of origin who has ventured into the land of feelings to pioneer and open this space for full acceptance. Learning to feel your feelings can feel scary, as it will bring you back to feeling the vulnerability you felt as a child. To feel like you are five years old again and that you could get in trouble is something you will move yourself through as you practice growing yourself up emotionally. This lesson's practice will assist you with doing that.

Shame can describe the overall state of our repressed negative emotions from childhood. You don't have to have experienced abuse to have been shamed as a child. In my system of Energy Profiling, I help you identify your true nature within a 4 Energy Types profiling system. From creating this body of work and studying its application to our self-identity, I've found that if we were not recognized for our true nature as children, or if we were disciplined for just being ourselves, we experience shame that subconsciously develops into a self-perception that we are not good enough. This false belief of not being enough, of lacking value as a human, has been a generational imprint for many generations in your family. You may be the first one in your family who has chosen to eradicate it. (To learn more about your specific Energy Type, see resources in the appendix.)

We often attempt to correct a sense of inadequacy in our adult lives with what we try to achieve. Because we don't feel "good enough," we subconsciously believe we have to "do more" to make up the difference. We become human doings rather than human beings. It is a common pattern to equate your self-worth to what you do and achieve in life. You know you have attached your self-worth to your life doings if you feel bad when you compare yourself to someone you believe does more or appears to be more accomplished than you. You might even try to find fault with this person, as that is the subconscious mind's effort to help you not feel so bad.

In today's world of social media, it is easy to experience a pattern of comparing, feeling bad, or avoiding feeling bad by judging the choices of others. Several years ago, I noticed my tendency to pass judgment on others' accomplishments and life pursuits when I read about them in various social media spaces. I knew that this was only hurtful to me and unnecessary. To prevent this from happening, I knew I needed to be less informed! It was really not any of my business what others chose to do with their lives. I also knew this was rooted in old energies of shame that I was healing in my life. So, until I could celebrate the lives and achievement of others, I needed to unplug from them and not follow them. I can now celebrate others because I have practiced and nurtured celebrating my true self and my worth. I am a being of affluence, ease, and joy, and so are you.

Here's another way to identify if your self-worth is attached to your doings: feeling inadequate and like a failure if you fall short or do not succeed at something. For example, can people give you feedback about your performance at work without you feeling personally attacked? If you are a full-time parent, do you compare yourself to others and feel less than the others you compare yourself to? Or do you feel better than they are because you find fault with them? The best method of eliminating a sense of worthlessness is to release your personal value from your life doings.

Because our sense of lack, shame, or inadequacy was established in childhood, we can compare our emotional energy to being like a child. I have referred to this part of ourselves as our "inner child" for many years now in my writing and teachings. The inner child represents our emotional energy, our unexpressed buried feelings that stay trapped until we acknowledge and express them.

I have found that expressing these feelings is as simple as doing the writing exercise I will offer you later in this lesson. You might be the only person your feelings will be expressed to, but they are being expressed, and feelings only need to be expressed and heard to be released to be able to heal.

For most adults, feeling their feelings is something they have had to learn in their adult experience. This is especially true for men, as having and expressing feelings were considered "unmanly" not so many decades ago. Many cultural stereotypes overlaid on humanity have suggested that feeling your emotions is somehow a human weakness. How many times do you apologize for tearing up over something in a good way? If you are a man, were you taught it wasn't manly to feel your feelings? Feeling safe to feel your feelings can take time. You need conscious practice to learn how to manage them so they don't manage you and get the best of you.

As part of the evolution of our consciousness, we are evolving the emotional aspects of ourselves. Until we explore the emotional energy field of our inner space and heal the generations of unexpressed fear and anger that reside there, it won't matter how much we explore outer space, as we will only create more war and terror out there! How do you know if you still carry repressed emotional energy? Take a moment to recall the last time you became emotionally upset, beyond what the experience may have justi-fied. That is the indicator that you have emotional energy to clear.

It is time for you to "feel" good about yourself just because you have a self. It is time to own the truth and adopt the beliefs, "I am worthwhile just because I exist. There is nothing I have to do to feel good about myself. I feel good about myself independent of my life doings."

Once you ground yourself in the energetic truth that you are enough, that truth abides in you and you never have to reconsider or question it again. Grounding yourself this way is like finding a stabilizing emotional center point that you never go off bal-ance from again. You might have an emotionally challenging day, yet you can stop relating your emotional ups and downs to your personal worth. You get to a place where you never question it. I know I am worthwhile. I feel I am worthwhile. I have been grounded and centered in this energy for over two decades now. The exercises in this week's lesson will assist you in creating this for yourself as well.

Are You Keeping Yourself Emotionally Safe and Limited?

If you were emotionally shamed and wounded in your child-hood, you most likely have the pattern in your adult life of keeping yourself emotionally safe. What that looks like is trying to prevent yourself from re-experiencing the feelings of shame and inade-quacy that you were forced to feel in your childhood.

In an effort to prevent feeling bad again you are also prevent-ing yourself from feeling as good as you are naturally designed to feel. In an effort to prevent feeling bad, you are also limiting what is possible for you in living a life of affluence, ease, and joy.

Filling your life experience with what is familiar and predictable to you keeps your potential from showing up. In an effort to keep yourself emotionally safe, you could be blocking what wants to show up from showing up. A student of mine shared the following:

"Once I learned I had this pattern, I could see very clearly where it was playing out in my life. I had experienced a very traumatic childhood and abuse and abandonment from my father. As an adult, I had created one relationship after another with men who were always more attracted to me than I was to them. I was in my mid-thirties when I had my emotional blinders removed to what I was doing. My inner child did not want to be hurt again, let down, and disappointed. In an effort to keep myself emotionally safe, I couldn't take the risk of attracting a man I would be strongly attracted to and even fall in love with because I didn't want to take the risk of being abandoned again. I kept filling my relationship space with what I really didn't want which kept the man of my dreams from showing up! Once I saw this pattern, Carol helped me clear the old energy and reframe my childhood experience in an energy that allowed me to now attract someone I was mutually attracted to. I am happy to say that I have been married 10 years to that man and we are now emotionally growing together in our partnership."

Consider the possibility that, along with repressed negative emotion, you carry repressed positive emotion from your childhood. If expressing emotion was not supported or acknowledged when you were growing up, you would have kept yourself in an emotionally neutral stance. Your joy (expressed as enthusiasm, laughter, outbursts, sparks of positivity and excitement) may have been shushed and silenced. Ironically, a parent who is emotionally wounded not only did not want to hear and feel what they saw as negative emotion, they did not want to hear and feel your positive emotion, as this could have been a trigger for them also.

As you free up the negative emotion you repressed as a child, you also free up the positive emotion you were not allowed to feel. How much joy is waiting to be felt in your life? How many things are trying to spark your repressed joy today? Pay attention and let yourself feel that joy. How exciting for you and all of us as you spread more joy, just by allowing yourself to feel it!

Emotional Addictions

The emotional patterns we become conditioned to feeling can turn into emotional addictions—states of emotional waves and vibrations that we subconsciously become dependent on feeling. For example, let's use the emotion of anger as a vibration you could be addicted to. If you have an anger addiction, you unknowingly keep re-creating experiences that provoke you to anger, just so you can feel the vibrations of anger. If you are addicted to sadness, you may recreate scenarios that provoke sadness on a routine basis just so you can get your "hit" of sadness. Maybe guilt is your emotional addiction. You could run the feeling of guilt every day if necessary, as you need it as a substitute for something else.

One of my students shares the following story of recognizing she has a pattern of feeling guilt every day and her "a-ha" about how to start shifting it:

"I feel guilty about everything. Even things I can't control, I still feel guilty. I did the visualization Carol recommends about visualizing you are with God and giving him your burdens in order to get a gift. I gave him my guilt. Guilt of not being the best daughter, wife, mother, employee, friend, scout leader, etc. He took my burden and replaced it with peace. Today I have peace. I have been able to say No this morning and not feel guilty. I have to take care of my needs and one of the things I have to learn is that it is ok to say No and not feel guilty. I am worthy, I am enough and I do deserve to want things in my life. Wow, what an a-ha! I want to be un-stuck, and in order to feel that, I must take time to realize what I want and to ask for what I want."

Your emotional body could be substituting negative and uncomfortable emotions as a source of false power and energy it needs to compensate for any limiting beliefs you still carry. Consider the possibility that if you lack confidence in your true, healthy power, anger will feel like a necessary substitute in order for you to have a sense of self-confidence, even if that confidence is false. Sadness may be a mechanism to get others to notice you, feel sorry for you, and offer support because you don't believe you deserve to be noticed and supported. Guilt is a catch-all emotion that will just keep you feeling bad about yourself and hiding so that you don't have to take responsibility or risks that may not work out. It's easier to feel guilty than to feel like you could fail.

How do you know if you have an emotional addiction? Notice any troubling emotions you are feeling on a consistent and regular basis—either daily, several times a week, or weekly. That is a good indication you have an addiction. How do you cure your emotional addiction? Do the practice steps in this week's lesson so that you can start to feel healthy, productive, and supportive emotions that will support you in creating emotional affluence.

Growing Up Emotionally

Emotional affluence looks like no longer carrying emotional energy from your childhood that is either repressed or (more often than not) triggered and getting the best of you and others. As you pioneer your emotional self and express your repressed feelings, you free yourself up to live the emotional *now*. As you continue to claim your emotional inner self, and stop carrying the feelings and the stories from the past, you will become emotionally free to feel your current feelings and the range of them as the experience of your life deems appropriate. You will become emotionally mature in present time, and have present-time feeling experiences.

As you grow up emotionally and begin to experience the appropriate feelings of your life, you will have a sustaining feeling of peace and well-being as your baseline emotional experience, even when you feel upset about something. This foundation becomes your emotional safety net to always bring you back to a place of emotional balance, allowing you to move through any upsetting emotion in a mature and timely way, being able to work things out if the reason for your upset involves others.

Learning emotional affluence and growing myself up emotionally are the areas I've had to spend the most time on through the years. Many times, I felt frustrated and angry that I had so much to feel that had gone unfelt in my childhood. I was one of the first wave of my generation to turn within and start healing the emotional energy field of myself. I began in 1987, with the work of John Bradshaw and his emphasis on healing the shame the inner child carried. As you do your emotional healing work, be patient with yourself. It won't require of you what it required of me, for the sheer fact that more and more people are connecting with and expressing their emotional selves. It's like Lewis and Clark; when they pioneered the western United States, it was a difficult journey, as few had gone before them. Nowadays, we can go any direction geographically with grace and ease on many paved roads and highways. Although we are in still in the early days of pioneering the emotional inner plains, we are beyond the Lewis and Clark stage of that experience. You do have some roads to travel on now.

As you move through this week's lesson, allow yourself to feel what is getting triggered and what is causing you to feel upset. You will be tempted to put a story on what you are feeling. Stop the stories and just feel your feelings. Breathe. Feel. Breathe some more. Feel some more. It is simple, yet can be uncomfortable. It is only uncomfortable because you attached the belief to those feelings as a child that it wasn't safe to feel them. It can even feel dangerous and scary to feel your feelings. Take time each day this week to feel your feelings.

Growing up emotionally is a process. How do we know when we have done enough emotional clearing and healing? I have had this question posed to me all through my coaching career as an energy therapist. It is often posed in a scenario like this client shares:

> *"I have done a lot of work on my family pattern of always creating a life of lack and struggle and also anger and resentment. I believed I had cleared the anger and resentment, but yesterday, out of the blue all this emotion came flooding back to me, and I sank again in the old feelings. How do we know when this energy is cleared for good?"*

The analogy of peeling an onion is perfect here! You heal in layers and stages. When you are peeling and healing that next layer, rather than say, "Why is this showing up again?" say, "Oh, I guess there's more healing to do." I've gotten really good at saying that! Although I still can get frustrated at times, due to feeling worn out and tired of feeling what I have to feel to clear these layers, I remind myself that it is a process. The good news is that even though you may have more layers to peel, you do not revert back to the previous layers.

The more and more you grow yourself up to create a state of emotional affluence, the more constant your states of joy become. Just remember, you may be the first one in your family line who is choosing to peel the onion. And what happens when you peel onions? You tear up a lot! Let the tears flow when needed. You will get to a point where the onion is peeled. Just make sure the emotions you are running are not an addiction.

As I experience more and more emotional affluence, I am free to feel a tremendous amount of joy for no apparent reason. That is when you know you have hit the space of emotional affluence. You feel joy, just for the sake of feeling joy. You no longer depend on life playing out a certain way, nor do you depend on a certain version of your story being intact. You can be going through either great times or challenging times and still feel joy. In challenging times, you can feel concern and worry, even fear, yet they don't take over. You move through those feelings to find yourself coming back to the center point of joy, the stable emotion you have tapped into as part of your truth.

When we choose to feel repressed, buried emotions that we are ready to heal, life will support us and set things up to trigger those emotions, so we can feel them.

The only way to achieve emotional affluence in the now is to feel and heal the repressed feeling of the past.

Tips for Raising Emotionally Affluent Children

We are still learning as parents to change the generational pattern of emotionally shutting down children.

In this week's Practice, I have you paying attention to the emotions of the children in your life. If you are a parent actively raising children in your home, this will be easy. If you are a grandparent, it would be good to spend some time with your grandchildren, if possible. If neither is an option for you, just take note of the activities that involve children and cater them to your situation.

What message are you sending to your children about their emotions? As we learn to honor our emotions as adults, we learn how to more fully honor the emotions of children. We can teach children to feel their feelings, but not to use their feelings to try and get their way. If we are still trying to repress our own feelings, we can get triggered by a child's feelings and our first reaction may be to get the child to turn off their feelings. As we free ourselves from repressed emotions, we are able to stay patient and calm during a child's emotional upsets and receive the inspiration needed in the moment to make the best decisions on behalf of the child. As we raise ourselves up to be emotionally affluent, we are able to raise emotionally affluent children who will not need to bury and repress their childhood feelings. Instead, our children can learn how to appropriately own their feelings, feel them, and express them with a parent's support. As you move forward into the Clear, Activate, and Practice sessions now, practice the tools to help you create the emotional affluence you are designed to experience, so you can support the children in your life in doing so, as well.

Emotional Affluence Step 1: CLEAR

Repeat the following clearing script out loud to clear and release your old emotional patterns of lack, pain, and struggle:

I am releasing any fear, anger, resentment, denial, avoidance, and anything else that would keep me from fully and 100% owning my emotional self.

I release the old programming that suggested that feeling my feelings is a weakness and shameful.

I clear any and all limiting and shaming messages that I may still carry in any and all parts of my being and body, from people I deemed authorities, who told me that I shouldn't be feeling what I am feeling.

I release it and let it go once and for all.

Emotional Affluence Step 2: ACTIVATE

Repeat the following activation script out loud to help you start creating emotional patterns of affluence, ease, and joy:

I am now choosing to open myself to the feelings I am ready to heal.

I choose to take time to do the emotional healing work that will allow me to grow up emotionally.

As I feel my feelings and heal my emotional self, every aspect of my life improves.

I am freeing up my body from having to store repressed emotions from my childhood.

Every day, in every way, I am more and more in touch with my feelings.

I am managing my feelings in a way that allows me to be honest with myself in how I feel, feel my feelings, and manage my emotional self with grace and ease.

I am grateful for the emotional affluence I am experiencing more and more each day.

Emotional Affluence Step 3: PRACTICE

For one week, do the following activities to help you create an inner foundation of emotional peace and well-being.

1. Your mantra for this lesson is: *There is nothing I have to do to feel good about myself. I feel good about myself, independent of my life doings.* Using a dry erase marker, write this mantra on your bathroom mirror and repeat it every morning.

2. Read the Clear and Activate scripts for emotional affluence each day in the morning.

3. Personal Inner Child Healing Exercise
   STEP ONE: Find a picture of yourself as a child, at approximately five years old (or at whatever age you feel drawn to). Look at it. Notice how small you were.

   STEP TWO: Request that your inner child (your emotional self) speak to you, by writing this statement with your dominant hand, "Dear Little Self, I would love to hear from you. Thank you for speaking to me today. What do you want to tell me this week?"

Carol Tuttle

STEP THREE: Switch to your non-dominant hand and write your inner child's response. Start by writing, "Dear Bigger Self," and then finish the statements below using automatic writing, giving no thought to what you are writing as you write. Just let it come out.

What I want you to know is

What I feel is

What I never was able to say is

I wish I were

What scares me is

What angers me is

What makes me happy is

What I want more than anything is to feel

4. Grounding to Your Emotional Truth

The following exercise will assist you in connecting your emotional energy to the truth that you are
enough, and there is nothing you have to "do" to be
enough. I recommend you record the following script
in your own voice using a recording app. Listen to this
short script every day of this week's practice.

With your eyes closed, turn your attention inward. Take
three deep breaths and relax. Turn your inner vision on
to see a spring of energy bubbling up inside of you in your
groin area, a powerful force of light coming up from the
bottom of your pelvic floor. You release this energetic
emotional spring that has always been there. You have

now turned on the flow of this emotional wellspring that feeds you daily with the feeling of "I am enough." You feel nourished and fulfilled. You feel peace and emotional well-being. You realize you are fed within emotionally and you will never need to look outside yourself to find emotional sustenance. Repeat the following:

I am constantly emotionally nourished.

I feel fulfilled.

I am peaceful.

I am sustained in well-being.

I am enough.

I feel my worth.

I am now connected to the energy of this emotional truth.

End of recording.

Dedicate time every day to be by yourself and turn your senses inward and find your emotional center. Once you find your center, you can always go back to it when you are feeling energetically unstable during the day. Any time you feel emotionally pulled off your center, as if you are being emotionally "taken out," close your eyes and connect with the wellspring of emotional peace and well-being within you. The more you do this, the more powerful this energy becomes. Eventually, it will be a constant supply of sustainable, peaceful energy streaming within you to support you in staying in the center point of emotional balance.

If you do not take time every day to connect with your own emotional center—your true energy which stabilizes a peaceful energy in you—you will be left to all the chatter going on in your head and many emotions from others that you may take on.

I recommend you download the Calm App and use it on your smart phone, iWatch, or other device to prompt you throughout the day to stop, breathe, and connect with your emotional center of peace.

5. For additional support this week, please use any of the Emotional Clearing Scripts found in the appendix.

Insights from Lesson 3

Emotional healing frees up the body to do what it is naturally designed to do: restore and heal.

LESSON 4

How to Create Physical Affluence

Teachings: Sustained Health & Vitality

As we move into the outer world and outer expression of yourself, we enter the experience of creating physical affluence. Physical affluence is the experience of your physical body being in balance, full of vitality. The body is the most energetically dense of the four energy fields of self: Spiritual, Mental, Emotional, and Physical. Because of this denser energy that vibrates more slowly, the body can take a little longer to shift its patterns. Be patient with your body. It's taken on a lot of stress for you and it needs you to become its ally now. There is a lot more potential for you on the physical experience of self that you have yet to realize and manifest.

The body's nature is to restore itself. It's a regenerative system that works without your conscious effort needing to be applied. There are countless chemical changes in your body every second. It's impossible for your conscious mind to influence or even participate in all those processes. When was the last time you had to think through the process of digesting your food? Your cells are dividing every second to replace all of the cells that die by the millions every day. Your body is an intricate system of biological programming that wants to be operating at its optimum level. It is a powerful, dynamic system that you need to learn how to get behind and support.

Numerous variables in today's world and lifestyle interfere with the body's capacity to stay healthy—from poor diets to lifestyle stressors, to negative talk about your body, repressed emotions that your body takes on for you, and inherited unresolved physical patterns that are passed from generation to generation. In most Western countries, we have accepted disease and declining health as something we have no control over. The good news is that on the physical level of self, your human nature has great power and healing when given the chance and the proper support to operate at its optimal level.

The first step in achieving the state of optimum physical health is believing it is possible. In this week's lesson, you will be supported in looking at and changing your thoughts and language around your body. The body has incredible resilience and incredible capacity to overcome interference and disturbances.

It's important to not skip TO this lesson, even if you feel your physical issues are the most powerfully presenting in your life. The physical energy field has a deep connection with the mental and emotional energies of ourselves. If we do not do the mental and emotional work first, we are not giving the body the chance to make a shift from the patterns of lack, pain, and struggle to a body of affluence, ease, and joy.

Your Body Is Listening to You

How do you talk about your body? What do you say about your body in your self-talk and the words you say to others? Do you view your body in a positive light or do you feel at odds with your body because your current physical experience is not the experience you want? From telling yourself you are fat, talking about how you are just getting old and your body is falling apart, to sharing your physical ailments as a sort of badge of honor, what you say internally and externally about your body either interferes with or aids your body's ability to heal. Take a moment and look at the day so far. What did your body hear you telling it? Changing how you think and speak to and about your body is one of the fastest, most inexpensive remedies that will free up your body's healing powers to help it restore itself to a healthy state.

Notice the language commonly used in the world of health care. It represents the language of lack, pain, and struggle:

I am fighting cancer.
I am struggling with chronic pain.
We have to win the war on drugs.
I am battling with my weight.
I am fighting this disease.

Violent metaphors that include words such as *fight, battle,* and *war* are common in the reference to disease and illness. We have adapted to this language and use it readily and frequently. Words hold vibrations, and we feed energy to what we focus on. Using violent references will create an interference to your body's capacity to heal and will add to the experience of lack, pain, and struggle at the physical level. It may inspire your mind to "win the fight," yet your body will be more powerfully aided by using positive metaphors that align you with the energy of affluence, ease, and joy.

Your Body Takes on Your Repressed Emotion

Along with negative thoughts and self-talk, if you have repressed any emotional energy, your body is taking it on for you.

Your personal energy system is a hierarchy, descending in vibrational frequency from the highest-vibration spiritual energy field down through the mental, emotional, then to the physical energy field. You could see it this way: your deeper, spirit self is always energetically intact and it first influences your mental energy, by flowing energy to new ways of thinking, insights, revelations, or changes of perception. This mental energy then moves down into your emotional field to either bring up old feelings that vibrate at a slower energy or enhance feelings of joy, depending on how emotionally whole you are. Then this energy moves into the physical body to help it cleanse and heal. If we are resistant to learning and understanding new paradigms and ways of being, or we have shut off our emotions, we become stagnant and the body takes the hit. When we are constantly flowing lack thinking and old repressed emotional wounding to the physical body, it has to create something with that energy. If we are not operating as a system of holistic balance, our bodies will create imbalance and disease. When we have a physical issue and we only address the physical symptoms, we miss the origin of where the energy comes from—the mental and emotional fields.

The body is a regenerative system that is designed to restore and heal, when freed to do so. If mental or emotional interferences create physical stress, the body can benefit from supportive resources that help clear this energy and free it up to achieve a state of balance. The Practice for this lesson and the Physical Clearing scripts found in the appendix will assist you in clearing the mental and emotional energy fields that influence your ability to experience physical affluence.

Inherited Physical Issues

Along with poor diets and lifestyle stressors, inherited and unresolved physical patterns may be the biggest cause of any disease you are experiencing. Consider the possibility that the current physical issue you may be dealing with can be traced back to your ancestors. Who else in your family had similar physical issues? You are probably not the author of the original physical disease and energetic imbalance that you are a carrier for, but you can be the one to resolve it and transmute the energy to allow you to create new patterns of health and vitality.

This is true for the back, leg, and foot issues that created a state of chronic pain in my life for four years. My father suffered from the same condition. In my commitment to clearing that old story, I was able to heal the beliefs and emotional patterns that my body carried from my ancestors, and also recognize and heal what I had chosen in my own beliefs and language that contributed to this chronic condition of daily pain.

In learning to support my body in its healing ability, I had to address both the "now" and "then" history of what I was experiencing. The "then" was the generational history of physical patterns in my family system that had never been healed. The "now" included the events and circumstances of my own life experience that had manifested in physical imbalances

As I kept "peeling the onion" of the origin of my pain in my own lifetime, a highly talented orthopedic cranial-sacral therapist discovered the original event that started to throw off my posture and balance. At 12 years old, I was hit in the head from the full swing of a baseball bat. My body started to compensate for the imbalances of that head trauma by adjusting my posture, so that by the time I was in my 50s, I walked five inches forward on the balls of my feet. My upper body had adjusted to prevent any upper body pain, and my lower body had taken the brunt of it for 43 years, until my back, lower limbs, and feet finally "blew out." I learned to address my physical issues by attracting the correct resources and support into my life to assist me in healing. Physical therapy, fitness, diet, and lifestyle changes supported me in creating healing and physical wellness over time.

Your Body Is the Doctor

Physical healing was new territory for me. Before I experienced chronic pain, I had successfully pioneered the landscape of my mental and emotional self and had experienced great healing in my inner world. But when my back, leg, and foot issues showed up, I exhausted numerous resources for well over the first year and got very little lasting results. It was at that time of frustration that I had an epiphany and a massive wake-up call that completely changed my perspective on physical healing.

One day, I was sitting at home feeling sorry for myself, tired, angry, frustrated at all the effort, time, and money I had applied in finding what would help me get well. I was practicing new beliefs about my body, I was changing the way I talked about it. Yet nothing much was changing. This is when I was told as clear as day:

"You are looking in the wrong place for help. There is not a resource outside of you that will fix your body. The resource IS your body. YOUR BODY IS THE DOCTOR. Any resource outside of you is only there to help support what your body already is designed to do—heal."

It had become my habit by this point to "look outside myself" for something to fix my body. I had to make "my body is the doctor" my new mantra to continually remind myself. Once I made this shift and really began to believe it and practice it, magic happened. I wasn't healed overnight. In fact, it took three more years! Did I still get angry, frustrated, and feel defeated? Yes, very much so, but I would meet that emotional space with patience and kindness as I moved through the experience.

How did I learn to listen to my body as the doctor? I started to talk to my body and learned to hear what it was telling me. Every time I reenacted the habit of looking for or depending on the next external resource to heal me, I would stop, turn my attention to my body and say, "You are the doctor, guide me to what you need to heal." My body taught me that it is wise and powerful. These simple steps of stopping, putting your attention on your body, asking for its feedback and listening to what it is telling you, will create a profound relationship with you and your body. How do you know what your body is telling you? You just will! You feel it in your gut! Just fake it until you start to sense something. You may not initially be able to hear and interpret your body's guidance, but give it time and keep doing these simple steps and I promise you, you will. Your body will start telling you how much sleep it wants, the types of food that will support it, the amount of alone and quiet down time it needs, the kind and amount of exercise that supports it. As you give your body that role and power, it puts out an energy that attracts to you the resources that will be beneficial for you. You will know which resources are supportive and you will know which resources you do not need to invest in. I have been listening closely to my body for nearly four years now, and a strong and clear connection has developed and will continue to develop. As a result of following my body's guidance, I was successful in healing a condition my 90-year-old father died with. I feel confident that you will find the answers and get the results you are seeking as you learn to trust your body as your doctor.

Making Pain Your Friend

Making pain your friend may feel and sound like an oxymoron to you. Why would you want to make friends with something you do not want? Wouldn't making friends with pain encourage it to stay in your life? As I started to make friends with my pain and believe that my body could fully restore itself, I learned useful things that allowed my body to heal.

Even though pain is meant to be a wake-up call that something is out of balance with our bodies, it is often treated like an unwelcome guest. All we want to do is get away from it or to have that guest leave as soon as possible. It may not seem like it at the time, but pain exists in our bodies as a way of getting our attention back to ourselves. Since your unwelcome guest is not going away, maybe it's time to befriend it and welcome what it has to teach you.

Find a quiet place to sit or lie down, inside or outside, wherever you feel completely safe and comfortable. Turn your attention toward your pain, wherever it is presenting in your body.

Locate the painful area (your head, neck, back, leg, or wherever). If you can, feel the boundaries of the pain: is it the whole leg, just in the thigh, or localized to just above the knee on the inside of your leg, etc.? Your headache may be just behind your right eye, or just over your left ear. Shift your awareness between painful areas and adjacent non-painful areas. Notice the differences. Let the non-painful parts "talk to" the painful parts. This is often enough to start the pain "moving" or "softening."

Now, forget the pain for a moment and focus on your breathing, your sense of your body connecting with the surface on which you are sitting or lying.

Now, localize the pain again. Notice a non-painful part of your body. Practice going back and forth between them. Come back to the pain and this time, "go into" it. Really try to feel it. You may be surprised that the pain morphs from physical to emotional (sadness, anger, fear, love) and back again. It may even change locations or be felt at multiple locations in your body.

When you really get to know your pain, because you have fully felt it and followed its movements in your body, it may eventually lessen in intensity and perhaps even disappear completely. Until that happens, make it your friend, and learn from it just like any good friend who will tell you the truth about yourself.

Along with visualizing the outcome of my pain going away several times a week, I began to attract into my life the resources that supported my body in the process of healing. As I look back, I see that each resource showed up at the perfect time as the next correct step in my healing. If you are experiencing chronic pain or health issues, open yourself up to the next correct resource coming into your life. You may not know what it is, but by befriending your pain and believing that your body can be supported, you can shift your mental and emotional energy to attract that resource into your life. As a result of my learning, I am grateful I have gone through my physical challenges, so that I can better help you achieve a physically affluent state of being.

A Medical Diagnosis Is Your Experience, Not Your Identity

You may be experiencing a physical ailment that comes with a medical diagnosis. Modern medicine is a diagnostic model. When you go to the doctor, your doctor will provide a diagnosis, as that is the model they are trained in, in order to advise you with a treatment plan.

Getting an accurate diagnosis can be a great relief, as it helps you to know what you are dealing with. The fine line in receiving that diagnosis is to not make it your identity and give your power away to it.

Certainly, some diagnoses can be more frightening than others. Being diagnosed with cancer or a terminal illness can be earth-shattering. It is important to feel your feelings, your anger, fear, confusion, and any other overwhelming emotions that might be presenting. As you move into this emotion, you free up your body to start finding answers to give you guidance. Your will to live needs to be empowered as you cross over from the unknown to a now-known diagnosis. More than ever, you need to dig deep to find your will and your body's will to recover and live to your fullest, whether you have a few short years or many more. You are still living. Do not let a frightening diagnosis end your life before your life truly ends. The one guarantee we all have is, we will die. Choose to live as fully as you can with the life lessons you are experiencing.

More than ever, people are beating the odds when it comes to healing or outliving the diagnosis of a terminal illness. More cancer survivors have turned into thrivers than ever before. It has been scientifically documented that an affluent mindset and emotional position contributes to your success to heal a terminal illness.[xiii] Take the term "terminal" and turn it toward the illness, rather than have that energy focused on terminating your life. In other words, take that energy and have it terminate the illness. Remember that energy obeys you. If a physical experience has been diagnosed as terminal, point that energy towards what you want to terminate. You want to terminate the physical imbalance you are experiencing—not yourself. A powerful affirmation to use is, "I am terminating this illness and coming back into my fully balanced and healthy physical state of being."

We can take on a diagnosis as our identity if we subconsciously need our physical ailments to try and help us meet some unmet emotional needs. Get really honest with yourself about any emotional needs that are met because of the way you experience your ailment. Do you need your ailment to feel like others care about you? Does it give you an identity that helps you feel like you belong somewhere? Were your parents more attentive and considerate of you when you were sick as a child? How is your physical ailment serving some value in your life? As long as you are using your body to serve any unmet emotional needs, you will not fully heal and allow your body to create an experience of affluence, ease, and joy.

Ask yourself the following questions to see if a medical diagnosis or physical ailment is hijacking your identity:

1. *Are you putting your plans and life on hold because of your physical condition?*

2. *Do you think first about your physical condition before anything else when making decisions about your daily, weekly, or life decisions?*

3. *Are you caught up in medication schedules, procedures, appointments, as the priority of your life?*

4. *Are you holding onto a diagnosis that may be keeping you stuck in re-creating what you don't want?*

5. *How quickly do you share your diagnosis or physical ailment with people you are meeting for the first time?*

6. *Are you receiving emotional value for keeping your diagnosis or physical ailment that you were not aware of?*

(And I need to add: Always consult a physician or a health care provider concerning any medical problem, issues, or conditions before undertaking any diet, health-related or lifestyle change program.)

A medical diagnosis is not your identity. It is an experience you are having at the physical level.

Three Areas to Support Physical Affluence

To help you create long-term physical affluence of health and vitality, I recommend supporting yourself in the following three areas:

- *Services and health care providers that aid physical affluence*
- *Movement and physical activity*
- *High-vibration food for your body*

A wide range of services and health care providers can aid you in creating physical affluence, from traditional to non-traditional resources. As you listen to your body as the doctor, you will attract and be led to the resources that are most supportive to you. I am not an extremist when it comes to going the route of either traditional medical care or alternative medical care. I believe there is a need and opportunity for both to aid us. Over the years, I have been led to and sought out both doctors and Western medicine, along with chiropractors and energy healers. At times, your body needs the aid of a medical specialist and medicine and other times it needs to be supported by more alternative and natural methods.

Modern medicine has saved two of my family members' lives. My son was born with pyloric stenosis and if he had not had surgery to open his pyloric valve at four weeks old, he would have died from starvation. My husband had a stroke when he was a young, 55-year-old man, and if he had not received the TPA medication to reduce side effects, he may not have been able to learn to speak again. The key to knowing which services support your needs is to learn to listen to your body, rather than the others' feedback or people you have placed in a role of authority in your life. Take their feedback and trust you will know what to do that is correct for you and your body.

Movement and physical activity consist of participating in a fitness program, daily or several times a week. What is your body drawn to at this time? It can change over the years as your physical needs vary from time to time.

The concepts of yin and yang are opposite but complementary energies that are worth considering in your balance of physical activity. Yin energy has a softer, inward-moving quality. For example, "yin"-based energy fitness experiences could look like walking, yoga, pilates, and other gentler recreation activities. Yang energy has a more forceful, outward-moving quality. So "yang"-based energy fitness experiences require more intensity and push from your body, such as running, cross-fit, HIIT, competitive sports, and more intense recreational activities. You could be drawn to hiking and choose to make it more yin or yang, depending on the intensity required of your body. Listen to your body's guidance, as it gives you feedback about whether you are most supported from yin or yang experiences. The balance may change over time, or require a blend of both.

When I became aware of the yin/yang difference in fitness options, I realized I was only experiencing yang energetic physical experiences. From running marathons over several years, then switching to triathlons and a lot of intense competitive tennis, I had pushed my body for years. I had adopted the common belief in the fitness world that if you are not pushing your body hard and exhausting it, you will not get long-term benefits. Along with the many benefits of healing I have experienced as a result of healing my lower body issues, my body taught me how to slow down and approach fitness in a more yin way. I now balance my fitness experience by listening to my body, and it tells me if it would benefit from a yin or yang experience. I now incorporate yoga, pilates, and a lot of walking in my day-to-day routines and my body is the healthiest it has ever been. Is your body asking for gentler yin experiences or more intense yang experiences right now—or a balance of both?

Consuming high-vibration food for your body is a key contributor to creating sustained health and vitality. In my lifetime, I have seen that we are shifting from a poor-quality diet of preserved and manufactured food to a more whole foods approach. We are going back to our roots when it comes to food. There is no such thing as a universally healthy diet. What's healthy for you may not be healthy for someone else. To find *your* uniquely healthy diet, you need to build your relationship with your body and become increasingly discerning about what it is telling you. As you do, you will begin to feel at a physical level what is correct to eat. Your body will begin to make your food choices, rather than your thinking mind.

Trust that your body wants to be healthy. It wants to perform well for you. It needs your support and belief in it and it will guide you in what to eat. As you listen more carefully, you will feed your body rather than your emotions. When you raise your physical vibration to a state of affluence, you naturally change the foods you eat. You are drawn to high-vibration foods, whole real foods, and clean eating. It's as if you can taste the low vibration in processed and manmade products and it no longer appeals to you.

High-vibration foods include: fruits, vegetables, grass-fed meats, eggs from cage-free chickens, healthy fats, nuts, legumes, whole grains, and low carb sweeteners made from plant-based foods. Think: Did this come from a living plant or animal that was treated kindly? (If you are vegetarian and believe that killing an animal is cruel, I honor your belief and trust you are following your own body's guidance.)

Low-vibration foods include: packaged and processed foods, regular and diet sodas, fast foods, white sugar, white flour. Think: Did it come out of a package with a list of ingredients I can't even pronounce or identify? Most of the products sold in the middle aisles of a modern-day grocery store are low-vibration foods.[xiv]

Looking at your current food regimen and diet choices, are you eating high-vibration foods or low-vibration foods?

Appreciating Your Body and Appearance

One of the phenomena and first-world problems women face in the modern era of fashion in Western culture is incessant body shaming. Men have also been drafted into this practice more recently, as a result of more exposure by the media of buff, well-built physical physiques, with an emphasis on bulk and massive muscles.

I have observed and studied this shame-based reference to bodies for the last 15 years. Women adopt a shame-based reference to their bodies in their early teens. They perceive that they are flawed because of beliefs that they are the wrong body shape and size, they are too fat, they age too quickly or that age diminishes beauty. They carry these perceptions with them throughout their lives. The entire fashion and beauty industry markets its products based on a woman believing her appearance is inadequate. All the ads motivate a woman to invest in an article of clothing or a beauty product to help her correct her misperceived flaws.

As a result of my years of studying the damaging effects of a shame-based beauty industry, I developed a system that I call *Dressing Your Truth,* to help women and men see and embrace their God-given beauty—both their inner and outer beauty. I have a lot of information online, along with a free course to help you shift this perspective about yourself. You can find more information in the appendix at the back of this book.

Women carry many misconceptions about themselves that keep them from experiencing physical affluence. Shirley's story is a common example.

Shirley struggled with self-defeating attitudes and a belief that she was ugly. She did not feel smart enough and she constantly berated her appearance. Even though she knew intellectually that the insults she told herself were not true, they still constantly played out in her self-talk and how she felt. After going through my free online *Dressing Your Truth* course, Shirley shared the following with me:

> *"Carol, I had no idea how much my negative view of my body and appearance was affecting me. I honestly just thought it was a bad habit. As a result of learning to dress my truth I have awakened to a beautiful understanding of who I am as a*

woman. I no longer depend on my appearance to feel good about myself, yet ironically, I look and feel better than I ever have. The compliments keep rolling in, and people say I look younger and healthier. My health is better, I understand my spouse more fully, I am full of confidence and living my life more fully than ever. Who would have thought that this could happen for a 65-year-old woman? I am not getting older, I am getting more real! Dressing Your Truth is definitely a big part of creating an affluent life—and a very affluent and practical wardrobe! Thank you, Shirley."

I hope you will take time to look into *Dressing Your Truth*, as it is a vital part of creating physical affluence for yourself. (You can find more information in the Resource section at the end of this book.)

Tips for Raising Physically Affluent Children

Gaining sound knowledge and creating solid habits to create physical affluence starts in our childhood. The changes you make now that support you in creating physical affluence will naturally be modeled and taught to your children. Parents play a significant role in supporting their children in getting supportive health care, proper fitness activities, and eating high-vibration foods. Start with yourself first and then enroll your children in these practices. Lead by example and make choices that can be sustained over longer periods of time, or you could end up teaching your children that the changes you are trying to make are just fads and trends, rather than long-term solutions for your entire family.

Physical Affluence Step 1: CLEAR

Repeat the following clearing script out loud to clear and release your old physical patterns of lack, pain, and struggle:

I am releasing any old beliefs, programming, habits, and lifestyle imprinting from my family and ancestors that are keeping me from creating physical affluence in the form of a healthy and vital body on all levels.

I am releasing from all cells, tissues, muscles, bones, fascia, organs, blood, and all body parts any false programming and limiting beliefs that my body carries from any and all experiences of my past.

I release any and all information and feedback that no longer serves my body's greatest good.

I clear any and all limiting and shaming messages that I may still carry in any and all parts of my body from people I deemed authorities.

I release and let it go once and for all.

Physical Affluence Step 2: ACTIVATE

Repeat the following activation script out loud to help you start creating physical patterns of affluence, ease, and joy:

I now choose to activate in all parts and functions of my body its pure and authentic expression of health and vitality.

I command my body to remember its blueprint of full and complete health.

I invite my body to start working as a whole system to come together and work as a holistic process to activate and restore the process of rejuvenation and regeneration.

I choose to make the changes necessary to support my body.

I am now listening to my body and it is telling me loud and clear the services, resources, fitness, and foods that will support it.

My body is strong and healthy.

I am grateful for the beautiful and loving relationship I have with my body.

I listen to my body and it continues to serve me as I fulfill my life purpose of creating an affluent life.

My body is whole and healed.

Physical Affluence Step 3: PRACTICE

For one week, do the following activities to help you create an outer foundation of sustained physical health and vitality.

1. Your mantra for this lesson is: *I am grateful for my strong and healthy body.* Using a dry erase marker, write this mantra on your bathroom mirror and repeat it every morning.

2. Read the Clear and Activate scripts for mental affluence each morning.

3. For five minutes each day, visualize your body as healthy and healed. Record the following script to start the visualization. Put a timer on for five minutes and keep your mind focused on your body being healthy and healed until the timer goes off.

    With your eyes closed, sit comfortably with your legs and arms uncrossed. Take five deep breaths, noticing both the inhale and the exhale. (Pause while you are taking the breaths.) Put your attention on the bottom of your feet, notice your ankles, calves, and knees. Now notice your thighs, your hips, your abdomen. Now notice your chest, shoulders, upper arm, elbow, lower arm, wrists and hands. Notice your neck, your chin, cheeks, nose, eyes, forehead. Put your attention on the top of your head. Take a deep breath and notice your whole body. Thank your body for how hard it's worked for you. Imagine wrapping your body in a blanket of healing green light. See yourself moving in your body free of any pain, ailment, or restriction of any kind. See your body the weight and size that is the healthiest for it. You are running happily through a field of flowers. Your body is strong and vital. You breathe in the fresh air, filling your lungs. See your body strong and completely restored to do what it was designed to do. See yourself doing something your body desires to do in its fully healthy state. Keep this visualization going until the five-minute timer goes off.

4. Your Body is Listening to You

   Pay attention to the thoughts and words you use this week in reference to your body and your health. At the end of the week, come back and answer these questions:

Were my thoughts and language in reference to my body and health positive or negative?

What I noticed is:

One thing that I can do differently is:

5. Making Pain Your Friend

Write a letter to your pain, ailment, or disease. Start with "Dear Pain," and then finish the sentences below to compose a letter that explores ways to turn pain into your friend. (If you are not dealing with pain specifically, use a variation to address your current physical concern: Dear Overweight Body, Dear Arthritis, Dear Diabetes, Dear Cancer, etc).

Dear _____,

I would like to start out by letting you know that you're the

You have shown me

You have left me feeling like

I've learned

Before you showed up, I didn't know

You have taught me

Thank you for

I hear from people all the time "I'm sorry" when I introduce you. I smile and say, "It's OK," because the person I've become is

You, _____, are my friend.

Love,

_____

6. Services, Fitness, Foods

As you listen to your body and refer to your body as the doctor, start to notice what it is telling you and guiding you to attract in regard to health care services, fitness practices, and foods that will support it in creating physical affluence. List here any insights you are receiving:

Health care resources my body is asking for:

Fitness practices that would support my body:

High-vibration foods my body wants:

For additional support, you can write to your body and ask it to share with you through the process of automatic writing. Automatic writing is a practice of just writing anything that comes to mind without taking time to think about it. You write as fast as the thoughts come into your mind. Some questions you can ask your body include:

Are there any health care services or practitioners that would be supportive to see?

How do you feel about fitness and working out?

Which fitness practices appeal to you?

Are there any foods you would like me to stop eating?

Which foods would you like more of?

Is there anything I am saying or doing to you that is hurtful to you?

Is there anything I am choosing now that would be supportive to stop doing?

What does your body have to say? Listen and then make adjustments.

7. Appearance
   Starting this week, choose to no longer look at yourself in the mirror and shame yourself by focusing on what you perceive as a flaw in your appearance. When you look in the mirror, just look at the whole you with appreciation and say *thank you.*

8. For additional support this week, please use any of the Physical Clearing Scripts found in the appendix.

Insights from Lesson 4

LESSON 5

How to Create Financial Affluence

Teachings: Having Lots of Money

Money is a constant in our lives. It can be a great blessing or feel like a life-long curse. It all depends on how much of it you have—and what you believe about how much you have. When you have plenty to spare, you feel it blesses your life with more choices and a sense of security. When you do not have enough, you feel a constant struggle, frustration, and even fear about it. People who have plenty of money feel in charge of their money. People who do not have enough money feel like money is in charge of them.

Of all six areas of mastering affluence, money is actually the easiest one to master. You may think it is the most difficult, but that is only because you have given that much of your power away to it.

From the thousands of people that I have helped to master financial affluence—both in private sessions and online courses—I have seen that everyone who creates struggle with money is playing off an old story that was created years before they were even born. Generational programming is the primary reason you may be struggling with not having enough money. That is easy to shift, but just like any area of mastering affluence, it takes practice to see it shift over time. Later in this lesson, we'll talk about how to write a new family story. In the meantime, as you read, consider looking deeper in your family line. What happened with money for your parents, your grandparents, or your other ancestor in the past? Have family members been praised for giving everything up and sacrificing for religious reasons? What about a family member who made a lot of money, then lost it, and never fully recovered it? What about a family member who became wealthy, created a more opulent lifestyle, and then was ostracized from the family?

The first thing to consider when creating financial affluence is to completely own your current story and creation with money, 100%. Take accountability and choose to own it. Even though the original story comes from your ancestors, you are the one creating the story now. What are you currently experiencing with money? Circle those that feel consistent with your experience:

- *Never having enough.*
- *Getting ahead financially only to go back to struggling again.*
- *Flowing a lot of money in income, yet never accumulating any savings and investments.*
- *Consistently spending more than you have, no matter how much money you bring in.*
- *Unexpected situations showing up that cost you money and set you back financially.*

- *Constantly worrying about running out of money no matter how much you have.*

What is your money story? Which patterns continue to repeat themselves when it comes to money in your life? Write your pattern here:

You may have been taught that money is not that important—it's only money. You may have been taught that you should never do anything just for the money, or that money is evil in some way. The truth is, money is important. We live at a time where money is a necessary commodity. We cannot take care of ourselves and our families without it. Money is a great resource that wants to bless our lives so that we are also able to bless others. Make money important in your life.

If you experience a lack of money, you have made money important for the wrong reasons. You have to think about it a lot, as you do not have enough to support you. Once you have financial affluence, you can come into balance with money by appreciating it, loving it, feeling gratitude for it, and not thinking about it so much!

In 1995, my husband and I had created a money story that played out as no income for 18 months, with $45,000 in credit card debt. In today's time, accounting for inflation, that debt would be equivalent to $75,000. That experience stopped us in our tracks and started us on a path to learn and understand the process of accountability, choice and effect, and the process of manifestation.

I have a distinct memory of thinking I couldn't be happy until I paid off all of this debt and had a predictable income again. One day, well into this story, I was standing in my bathroom and I heard God whisper to me, "You will not be out of debt and have an income until you learn how to be happy the way things are. That is your lesson—that happiness is not tied to money."

I accepted my lesson and went about practicing true happiness. I had a rule for myself. Every time I stressed about not having money, I would quickly change my thoughts to what I did have. I practiced happiness for several months. I learned my happiness lesson well. What I didn't know was that there was another powerful lesson built into the happiness lesson! The lesson was that when you detach your emotions and your spirituality from money, money has more freedom to flow and accumulate in your life. I started to become aware that money is just a resource. It is a neutral resource that is an exchange of energy that I use nearly every day to exchange for services and goods. It had nothing to do with my happiness, my self-worth, or my spirituality. It's a tool.

It's been over 20 years since my husband and I started to apply financial affluence practices in our day-to-day lives. Does it work? Yes, we have gone from no income and massive credit card debt to starting and building a multi-million-dollar business with the financial freedom that supports our chosen lifestyle.

Did you know that people with a lot of money do not think as much about money as people who do not have enough money?

What Is Financial Affluence to YOU?

It's common practice for teachers of the Law of Attraction to represent financial affluence exclusively as having millions of dollars. This is not necessarily helpful, nor is it true for every person. From the earliest money training sessions I offered, I encouraged people to tap into their soul purpose when it came to money. Not everyone is destined to be a multi-millionaire, yet everyone has the potential destiny of having enough money to spare to fulfill their threefold soul purpose experience that I introduced earlier in this book: enough money to support you in the lessons you came to learn, enough money to support you in the experiences you are meant to have, and enough money to support you in the service you are here to give.

I am a big believer that the more money you have, the bigger difference you can make on the planet. More and more, we are seeing the wealth of the private community being invested in making a difference in the world. Bill and Melinda Gates are a great example of using their wealth to improve the quality of life in many countries. Affluent people are the ones solving the global problems of poverty, water, hunger, lack of education—a role we used to solely depend on governments to fulfill. What problem or issue are you meant to solve as an affluent person?

Why Are You Still Experiencing Lack with Money?

If what I am sharing with you rings true, then why are you still experiencing a lack of money? Why does this pattern keep showing up for you? Because you are not aware of the little things you think and say every day that keep you creating what you don't want with money. Negative money beliefs run like a hidden software program, sabotaging your best intents. They are the small "voices" in your head that actually override what you would like to believe but don't. What goes on in your subconscious wields much power, perhaps even more so than your conscious mind.

What I learned during those first years of practicing financial affluence gave me a foundation that allowed me to apply the same thinking and practices to every area of my life. The lack of money got my attention to enroll me in what has become a game of mastery in all six areas of affluence that we are covering in this book. Let it become that foundation for you, as well. Let mastering affluence become a lifestyle, rather than a self-help technique that you practice for a while and abandon. If Jon and I had abandoned the practice of creating financial affluence once we were out of debt, I doubt we would have gone on to create what we have created with money and the other five areas of our lives. Also, the chance of reverting back to old ways and landing back in debt again was highly probable if we had not committed to the long-haul learning. I was committed to creating financial freedom, even if it took 20 years. I can honestly say that what I started practicing in 1995 has become a lifestyle habit that is the way I live. I want that for you as well, as everyone deserves to be free of their struggle with money.

Another powerful reason you are still creating lack of money is an old energetic generational story. If no one shifts the energy of an old story, you just get born into it and create your modern-day version of getting by and living in lack. Your ancestors most likely came from a story of having to get by. In past cultures of power and hierarchy, people with money ruled and you could only obtain that social class if you were born into it. Your money roots have centuries of old programming of lack and struggle with money. Your more recent ancestors of the last 100 years did have more opportunity to change the story, and some may have done so, but they were most likely still rooted in the belief that money was evil and going without was more spiritual. For example, if your ancestors lived in the United States in the 1940s, they may have been hit by the Great Depression and no one has cleaned up and re-patterned the energy of the family financial trauma. Those patterns are no longer consistent with the choices available today.

What are these old beliefs and patterns? Let's look at some of the most common conscious or subconscious beliefs that have been passed down generationally about money. As you read, circle those that are still showing up in your experience. This will help you recognize which generational patterns you are ready to clear. It's time to let money be an affluent resource that supports you.

1. OLD BELIEF: Money is evil.

Money has been given a bad rap for centuries. The money-is-evil storyline has been handed down for generations. Did you hear this, or something like it, in your family growing up? Not only was going without required in the past, but there was a time in your ancestors' cultural time period where the common people of the world could have been considered more spiritual and humble. Unfortunately, there is also a long history in humanity of people with wealth doing evil and inhuman things. But it was the people using the resource of money in evil ways—not the money itself doing anything evil. Money is a neutral energy. We project our perceptions onto it and we can use it as a tool to make choices with. Money has no morality. The person with the money projects their morality onto money. We now have opportunities for our own will and choice to determine how we want to experience wealth and success. We get to choose if our wealth and success will make a difference or spread suffering to others.

There has never been more freedom to decide how you want to play with money. It's really up to you. Having more money is not going to turn you into an evil, worldly person. It will just allow you more choices. You will be in charge of your morality, not money. I had a little chat with the energy of money and it is fed up with being the bad guy! Money now wants to be the good guy in our lives. It wants to help you and help this world. Start shifting your beliefs and emotions around money so that money can work for you.

Let's take a look at some other references about money you most likely heard from your parents or grandparents that influenced your original perception and opinion of money. Circle the ones that you heard growing up:

- *Money is the root of all evil.*
- *Money doesn't grow on trees.*
- *You have to work hard for money.*
- *Money doesn't come easily.*
- *People with money are evil.*
- *Money can't buy happiness.*
- *Money is in short supply.*
- *We never have enough money.*
- *The rich get richer, the poor get poorer.*
- *Our family has never been rich.*
- *It's selfish to want a lot of money.*

And the number #1 most-expressed phrase about money in our modern-day culture that keeps you financially poor: "I CAN'T AFFORD IT." Which of these lies are you still believing, either consciously or subconsciously about money?

2. OLD BELIEF: I can't afford it.

The most common phrase that keeps people creating lack and struggle with money is the go-to phrase: "I can't afford it." How many times have you said this phrase in the past week? It's a common habit and it feels correct to say it. Yet, every time you declare this, your energy puts out the message, "Keep me in a state of not being able to afford what I want." Most likely, you heard this phrase frequently from your parents.

I am often asked, "But Carol, what if I really can't afford what I want?" My answer: Then start pretending you can. It's a game that you play with your mind and emotions. You have a great imagination, and the rule of manifesting what you want more of is to focus on it and get excited about it. That does not mean you move into action and make a purchase if you do not have the money. Replace the phrase, "I can't afford it," with this powerful substitute that sets your energy up to attract more money:

"I can afford to believe in it, and I am allowing the money to show up for me"

3. OLD BELIEF: I can't have that because I don't have the money.

One of the leading habits that is keeping you from flowing and accumulating more money is a habit you engage in unknowingly on a regular basis. In fact, there is a good chance you have even experienced this well-developed habit in the past week. It is the practice of wanting something in your life (such as an experience, a learning opportunity, an item, whatever you're drawn to) and quickly telling yourself you cannot have it because you do not have the money. Before you are ever fully open to the possibility, you shut it down because of money.

The error is that you probably do have the money for most things you use this strategy for. You are just using this tactic to keep yourself from spending the money. At other times, you use this tactic honestly, as you may not have the funds for some of the bigger things and experiences you would like to have in your life.

Either way, you pay a big price for using this habit, as it stops the energetic flow of money. The cause and effect this practice creates in your personal energetic offering is closing your energy to more financial flow and accumulation. In fact, start to notice your personal energy when you have this response. You will feel your energy drop and close and you will be left to feel a state of lack.

Let's paint a picture of what this looks and feels like in daily practice. Think of something you wanted or were attracted to recently. Something bigger, such as a trip or larger purchase. Let's imagine you hear about a friend who is going on a great vacation, something you would love to do. Imagine you immediately have the thought and the feeling, *I don't have the money,* or *I shouldn't spend money like that,* or *I wish I could do that but there is no money for it.* Even if your current money reality makes that an accurate conclusion, notice what this does to your energy. You feel disappointed, maybe resentful. You feel powerless and held back from what you really want because of money. In that situation, you give all the power of manifestation to an inanimate object—money. Money doesn't have the power to decide if you can go on a vacation, yet you have given it that role in the moment of your reaction. You energetically turn off the faucet of financial flow every time you react this way.

Let's take the same scenario. Your friend tells you about a great vacation they are going on, and it sparks in you a feeling of wanting that also. Rather than immediately shifting your thoughts and feelings towards the "no money" reaction, try this. Tell your friend how great that sounds. In fact, you love the idea so much you are going to consider it for yourself. You tell yourself,

I would really love to do that, and you start to daydream about how much fun it would be. You tell yourself, *I can have that, too. I can afford to believe that if it is correct for me, the money will show up to support me in having this experience.* Notice how you feel while saying those positive and supportive thoughts and perceptions. What role does money have now? A supportive role rather than a controlling role. And since money responds first to your energy, the signal you put out in to the world, this signal is going to keep the financial flow faucet open, on, and much more powerful. To increase your flow of money, it is important to keep the faucet on.

When my husband and I started to practice this new response, we were able to pay off our credit card debt within 18 months. We would catch each other turning off the faucet and kindly remind each other, "Keep the faucet on!"

4. OLD BELIEF: Wealthy people are bad/evil/selfish/etc.

If you are judging wealthy people, then forget about flowing more money. You don't want to be one of those people, so subconsciously, you will not allow yourself to create financial affluence. Do you still have threads of the belief that rich people are evil? Do you believe that people with lots of money are worldly? The truth is, what other people choose to do with their money is none of your business! Make your accumulation of more money *your* business and let other people take care of their own money business.

I had a thorough teaching of this lesson in 1996, when I was standing in my driveway and my neighbor drove up in a new Mercedes Benz. I was furious. How dare they strut around in their luxury car? We were still in our debt phase and had not yet acquired steady income flow (and still working on the happiness lesson) when I stood there, really bugged that they had the money for this luxury car and I did not. The judgment energy was flying.

Once again, God whispered to me, "Carol, as long as you judge others for having money, you will not create your own." Whoa! Got it, God. It hit me like a load of bricks. Of course I wouldn't allow myself to create wealth and financial affluence. If I did that, I ran the risk of someone judging me! And I certainly wanted to fit in and not stand out in any way, shape, or form! That lesson came in so powerfully, I have not had another negative thought about anyone who has a lot of money. And before I walked into the house, I even blessed everybody in our neighborhood with a new Mercedes Benz!

Let's all be wealthy, rather than just some of us. Pray for others to prosper and thrive. Keeping yourself poor and in lack is not helping anyone and will not make it fairer for other people who have less than you. In order to stop judging others' money business, you need to stop comparing or talking about your loved ones' experience with money and what choices they make with it. Focus on what you want to create and let others create their own experience with money.

5. OLD BELIEF: I'm not worthy of having more money.

A student of my online course, The 30-Day Money Cure, shared the following story with me:

"My husband and I wanted to buy our first house, but I realized I didn't feel worthy of attaining a home I love. My worthiness triggers displayed by being concerned that we would not have enough money to get the house I wanted. So, I followed the principles Carol teaches and that same year we confidently bought our first house! But then, I realized I didn't feel worthy of fixing it up to be "our" house. I worried how long it would take to earn the money necessary for the projects. So I've continued to work on my worthiness triggers. I'm thankful to have fewer and fewer triggers. And we've earned more money than we ever have in our lives! I'm so excited and GRATEFUL! Thank you, Carol, for your teachings. My word for 2018 is #Manifest. And thanks to Carol Tuttle, my family and I are manifesting more financial affluence than ever!

It's appropriate and timely that you release your experience of money from being entangled with your morality, spirituality, and worthiness as a person. That is an old, old program. You are worthy, you were born worthy and money does not create or negate how much you are worth. Yes, in most experiences with money, there is an action step involved. But you cannot flow and accumulate more money just by being worthy.

Fine-tuning affluence in your physical, outer world requires what is referred to as the *Be, Do, Have* approach.[xv] In this world, some people assume they need to *have* a certain amount of money in order to *do* certain things, and then they will *be* happy. But they've got it backward. You need to work the other way around and start with *being* first. To do this, pretend you are wealthy in your thoughts and feelings. Allow your inner being to own it, to BE wealthy. What does that feel like? How does your energy lift when you own the idea that you are *being* wealthy? Once you have grounded that experience of being, thoughts will come to your mind of the next correct steps to take. Act on them. DO what you are then inspired to do to create more money. As you live out that process of being and doing first, the result will be that you HAVE lots of money.

6. OLD BELIEF: You are only doing it for the money!

When my business started becoming financially successful, I started to receive comments that suggested I was only doing what I was doing for the money! I had to laugh at that feedback, as what I have done in my online entrepreneurial business pursuits have not been easy. I'd say to myself, "You've got to be kidding me! If I were working only for the money, I'd be selling high-level real estate properties!" If I had not felt called to do what I do in my business and work career, I am pretty sure I would have abandoned it because it wasn't always profitable. But even if it were true that I had created my business only for the money, would that be a bad thing? Why *not* do something purely for the purpose of creating an increase of money in your life? What does that bring up for you to consider that you are purely doing something for the sake of having more money?

Through the years, as I have cleared out my old ancestral programming about money, I have let go of the judgment that doing something purely for more money somehow makes you a less spiritual person. I have come to appreciate money so much and feel so much gratitude for the choices it allows me. I am okay if someone does something just for money. Is it okay for *you* to do something just for the money? You may never need to because we live at a time when we can blend a purposeful cause with making money, but let yourself get there in your beliefs and feelings so that you can completely free money up to be just what it is—an energetic resource and tool.

If you are a business owner like me, in order to be successful in business it's important to adapt the belief, "The thing that I do for business makes money, and that is what supports me in being able to help more people." You will only have a business if you create something profitable, so that you are sustainable enough to reach more people. Money keeps you in business and is the engine that allows you more choices to do good in the world.

Money is an energy of appreciation. We give money to people in exchange for goods and services that we appreciate. We can use money to provide things and experiences that others appreciate. Start to appreciate what money can help you create. It is a tool and a resource meant to be used to help you with your threefold soul purpose of lessons to learn, experiences to have, and service to give. Finish this sentence, "What I appreciate about money is:

In my online course, The 30-Day Money Cure, I invite students to really delve into what they appreciate about money. Notice that we use the word *appreciate* a lot in the experience of money. We want money to appreciate for us, which refers to our money growing.

As you start to really appreciate money,
money will start appreciating for you!

One of my Money Cure students shared the following insight in the process of doing their writing exercise:

What I noticed was that I started writing my responses to what I appreciate about money and all of them started with "money allows me to" or "money gives me." I realized that this phrasing was indicative that money is still very much in the position of power. I essentially equate it with a withholding parent who gives it when and if they choose to, and I am at its mercy. So I am changing my responses to begin with something like "I appreciate money because I choose to use it to..." Words matter!

When we are living in the energy of affluence,

things show up effortlessly. You'll be saying:

Things come out of the woodwork.

They just land in my lap!

It's like it's raining exactly what I need.

People are thirsty for what I have.

Does All This Mean We No Longer Need to Work for What We Want?

I hear this question quite often when students start to learn and practice principles of financial affluence. For example, a Money Cure student phrased this question to me as follows:

"It hasn't settled well with me that we're collectively believing that we no longer need to work for our money. Maybe I'm misinterpreting but it seems like hard work is getting a bad rap here. I love a little hard work! I love the sense of accomplishment I feel when I complete something. We all need to ACT! It can be in the form of a little hard work, or even just focus and persistence."

Two fellow students responded so clearly that I'll share their insight with you:

"I don't think that's what is being taught at all. I see Carol as an extremely hard worker, so I really don't think that's what she is saying. I think it's the belief that money only comes through hard work, which is incorrect. The belief that we have to struggle and worry in order to survive is no longer our reality on this planet, because it is old programming. That's the message I have been receiving."

"I totally see what you're saying, but what I am understanding here is that we can choose to focus on gratitude and allowing more good to come into our lives through sustaining a higher vibration and have more success than we ever can as we struggle

and worry and continue to believe that things are difficult to come by, which actually repels the things we want (money being one of those things) from us. And the way I see it is, as I free myself from the constant worry and struggle and false beliefs surrounding money, then I can reallocate that energy into my actual true purpose and what God placed me here to do."

There's nothing wrong with hard work. A job well done can be so satisfying! But consider the possibility that hard work is not the *only* way that money can come to you. If you unhook money from that requirement, you open yourself up to many other opportunities and possibilities. How many ways can money come to you? It will be exciting for you to find out!

As you progress in creating financial affluence in your life, you create freedom and choices that you have not had before. Money is a tool that creates more choices for you. I believe you will be inspired in how to use the wonderful and powerful tool of money to bless your life and the lives of others. This Money Cure student shared it beautifully:

"I have found, that I am most joyful and fulfilled when I use my affluence to support my individual purpose to help make the world a better place through serving others. We can be led to work that isn't drudgery when we are living true to our purpose. And we are never too old, it is never too late, to discover our purpose. Our purpose adds value to the world. I have an expanding, joyful, timeless feeling inside my body when I am doing the work that is linked to my purpose. Those are just a couple of ways I know

my purpose. Whatever your belief system, pray, put it out there, whatever, for the Higher Power to help you see your purpose and live it!!"

Flow and Accumulation Make You Rich

Along with your energy's ability to affect the flow of money, your energy also affects the accumulation of money. Together, both flow and accumulation create wealth. Wealthy people flow a lot of money and they also accumulate a lot of money.

What are your patterns of accumulating money? How much do you have right now in savings or investments? Have you ever had over $5,000 in savings? If you accumulate money, does something show up in your life that requires you to spend it? Do you run the pattern that no matter how much you make, you never get ahead? That means you have a weak accumulation energy and you need to strengthen your energy's "stickiness" with money. This can be done with a simple visualization technique I will teach you in this week's Practice.

And remember the *Be, Do, Have* steps? First you need to Be in the energy of, "I flow and accumulate a lot of money." Then, you need to follow the inspired action that moves you to Do what helps flow money. If you stay in that energy and you do what you are inspired to do, then you will Have a lot of money flowing to you and accumulating!

Creating Your Own Personal Economy

With today's extensive news channels and media options, we have the opportunity to hear a lot of news about the nation's economy. Wherever you live in the world, you can choose to be a part of the energy of the collective economy that is represented in news stories, or you can choose your independent experience by creating your own affluence in your personal economy. There is evidence that this is possible, as no matter the state of the nation's economy, there are always people who are wealthy. Even during the Great Depression, certain people thrived financially.

The first step in creating an affluent person's economy is deciding you can and you will experience that. It will be important to not align yourself with the energy of the collective economy. This can be achieved by following these steps:

1. Refrain from watching and listening to news stories about the national economy. Your mind will be tempted to join the story. When you mentally agree with the story you are being told, your energy aligns to create that outcome.

2. Refrain from talking to others about the collective economy and how bad or great it is. Remember, you are creating your own personal economy, so it has nothing to do with what is going on nationally.

3. Choose to talk about how great your personal economy is going. During the collective economic slump that was

referred to as a global financial crisis between 2007—2008, my business grew and was very profitable. I know that choosing to create my own personal economy was a big reason we experienced this financial success. If you chose to talk about the national financial crisis, you chose to create that in your personal reality.

4. Avoid the tendency to think, "I have to be aware of this so I am prepared in case something happens." Preparing for a personal financial crisis is more likely to manifest a financial crisis. I think the best way to prepare for sustaining yourself in case of a national financial crisis is by creating financial affluence, no matter what is going on for the collective experience.

Be consistent in your Practice this week, as the activities will support you in beginning or continuing to create your own personal economy.

Write Your New Family Story with Money

Take a look at your ancestors' stories with money. What were your parents' stories and patterns with money? Are you still living any of them out currently? What about your grandparents or Uncle Joe or Aunt Susie? What traces of your family's money stories are still manifesting in your story?

What did you live in your family of origin when it came to money? Those are big clues to the generational patterns waiting for you to clear. If your family experienced challenges, it's okay to acknowledge them. Be honest about the patterns you grew up with, like this student of mine:

> *"When I was a child, my dad used to get angry and yell at me when I asked for money. He always made me feel like I wasn't worth spending money on. We often heard him say, "If it weren't for you kids, I'd be a rich man. I'd have a lot of money to do whatever I wanted." When I was a teen and had a job, my stash box always had less money than the last time I counted it. I blamed my brothers for stealing my money, 'til I caught my dad red handed in my stash box taking my money. I was angry at him for taking my money and for never owning up to it when I blamed my brothers and for all the times I was short of the money I needed to pay for something. I am breathing deep, forgiving my dad and releasing the fear of running short of money and not being able to fulfill my commitments."*

No matter what patterns of lack, pain, or struggle you've experienced, they can stop today, right now. Your bank account won't change overnight. Yet, if you turn the practices I teach in this lesson into lifestyle habits, your physical experience with money will change in time for good.

Remember the story of my husband's great-great-grandfather who gave up his lucrative brick mason business to follow God? Once Jon and I uncovered that juicy lack-of-money story, we were on our way. First, we shifted the energy, and that continued to shift the way our physical world played out when it came to money. It works. I've seen it happen over and over. Let it work for you. You can either keep doing what you are doing and keep experiencing the same old thing, which turns in to the same old thing with not enough money 20 years from now, or you can change what you are doing and your life right now with money will change for good.

Money does not make you a good or bad person.
It just makes you more of who you already are.

Tips for Raising Financially Affluent Children

My number one tip is to stop saying "We can't afford it" to your children. Jon and I stopped this when our children were in grade school and it was one of the most powerful changes we could make in raising financially affluent children. So, what do you do when you are at the grocery store and your child is relentless in asking you to buy something? Be relentless in saying, "No, I do not want to use our money for that right now." And then invite your child to create a flow of money so they can be the one to make the purchase. I would tell our kids, "That is great that you want that. I am not going to use our money on that. I support you in creating the money to give yourself those choices."

It is also important to let go of the lack of money being a morality lesson for your children. If you still have the belief that going without money somehow makes us better people, you could have your grown children living with you longer than you would like or is best for them! And what's best for them is what you'll be creating for yourself.

Remove all the lack and limiting money language from your vocabulary. Teach your children that money is a tool, a resource that supports and blesses our lives. We are the creators of our money experience and you want to teach them how to create financial affluence. Show forth appreciation for money to your children and your money will appreciate for you in return.

Ask yourself: What is one thing I can do differently when it comes to my experience with money that would support my children in creating financial affluence for their entire lives? Pay attention to what comes to mind. Choose to raise financially affluent children, rather than pass on to the next generation the family money stories and practices that keep them poor and living in lack when it comes to money. Teach them how to be good, civil people. Teach them that money does not have the power to make us good or bad; it gives us more choices. Teach them how to use money as a tool to make a difference in the world.

Financial Affluence Step 1: CLEAR

Repeat the following clearing script out loud to clear and release your old financial beliefs and patterns of lack, pain, and struggle:

I now choose to release and clear from my life (and the lives of my ancestors, as far back as I need to go), all of the beliefs, perceptions, attitudes, opinions, references, judgments, and practices that have created financial struggle and a lack of money.

I free myself from all inherited influences that may have caused me to attach my spirituality and my self-worth to money.

I free myself from any and all attachments I have given money including:

- *Money is more powerful than me.*
- *I don't have a say in how much I can flow and accumulate.*
- *Money is a struggle.*

I ask that the accumulative energy that has created a lack of money from all of the times I have declared "I can't afford it" be cleared.

I am now free to create financial affluence and write my new story with money.

Financial Affluence Step 2: ACTIVATE

Repeat the following activation script out loud to help you start creating financial patterns of affluence, ease, and joy:

I love money and money loves me!

I now choose to activate my full potential with flowing and accumulating money.

I am a money magnet.

I now have a healthy and friendly relationship with money.

Money loves to support me.

I appreciate all of the choices available to me as a result of the money I have.

I am committed to creating new habits and practices that support me in creating financial affluence for the rest of my life.

Financial Affluence Step 3: PRACTICE

For one week, do the following activities to help you create a strong foundation of financial affluence in your outer world.

1. Your mantra for this lesson is: *I love money and money loves me.* Using a dry erase marker, write this mantra on your bathroom mirror and repeat it every morning.

2. Read the Clear and Activate scripts for financial affluence each day in the morning.

3. Focus on changing your thoughts and language around money this week, from statements of lack to statements of abundance. Circle the statements below that you say frequently. Note the new statement and use it in place of the old one:

PHRASES OF LACK	PHRASES OF FINANCIAL AFFLUENCE
Money is just a pain in the butt.	Money is a joy to my heart.
You have to earn it.	You have to be open to receive it.
I can't afford it.	I can afford to believe in it and I am allowing the money to show up for me.
Money is so hard to come by.	Money is easy to come by.
You have to work hard to get ahead.	You have to believe and follow inspired action and you will get ahead.

PHRASES OF LACK	PHRASES OF FINANCIAL AFFLUENCE
Money is filthy and dirty.	Money is beautiful.
Money is evil.	Money is a neutral resource.
Money is in short supply.	Money is in abundant supply.
Money goes out faster than it comes in.	I always have more money coming in than going out.
The cost of living is so high that it is impossible to keep up.	I always have enough and to spare.
A penny saved is a penny earned.	A penny is a penny.
You never know when the rainy day will come.	I am always financially prepared and secure.
Money only comes from hard work.	Money first comes from what I believe about money.
Rich people are greedy and dishonest.	Rich people are whoever they choose to be.
Having money makes you less spiritual.	I am as spiritual as I choose to be.
It's easier to spend than to save money.	I flow and accumulate a lot of money.
Good opportunities are hard to come by.	Great opportunities come to me frequently and easily.
I do not deserve success.	Everyone deserves success, including me.

PHRASES OF LACK	PHRASES OF FINANCIAL AFFLUENCE
Everyone else comes first.	As I put myself first, I am able to serve others.
I can't handle or manage money well.	I create the support I need to manage money successfully.

4. Play the $500 bill game. Every day this week, imagine you have $500 dollars in your wallet that you have to use by the end of the day. You cannot save it. You have to make a decision and spend it on something. Put a reminder in your phone or planner that says: Spend today's $500. List here what you spent your $500 on:

Day 1:

Day 2:

Day 3:

Day 4:

Day 5:

Day 6:

Day 7:

5. Flow and Accumulation Visualization. Record this 60-second visualization and listen to it at least three times this week:

Imagine you are standing in a river about knee deep and the water is flowing toward you. The water turns into dollars bills, coins, and the energy of money, all moving and flowing to you. You just stand there and feel the energy of money flowing to you from every direction. It's pouring into your life. You look above you and there is a faucet that is open and flowing in more money. You turn around and no matter what direction you face, the energy of money is always flowing directly to you. It begins to accumulate and grows and grows underneath you. It sticks to you all over your body, and there is a growing mound of money beneath you. You feel the support of it under your feet. You are like a magnet that constantly flows money and that money sticks and accumulates. You sit on the mound and throw the money up in the air and see yourself playing with it. It is there to support you living an affluent life.

6. Write Your New Family Story with Money

What patterns do you want to experience with money? Write them down. Paint a picture of what life looks like with this new family story, by finishing this sentence. I am grateful that my family and I are now experiencing the following with money:

7. For additional support this week please use any of the Financial Clearing Scripts found in the appendix.

Insights from Lesson 5

How to Create Relationship Affluence

Teachings: Harmonious & Collaborative Intimate Relationships

In this lesson, I will refer to partner relationships from my experience as a married female in a heterosexual, sexually monogamous relationship. If you have a different relationship experience, please make adaptations to what I share to fit your lifestyle choices and values. I accept all people's experience, yet I can only teach from my own experience on how I created affluence in my relationship with my husband.

Relationships are going through a major shift in how we experience them. For centuries, relationships have been energetically configured in the energy of hierarchy. In our intimate relationships in most cultures, we have experienced this as the male being the dominant partner in the relationship and the female being the subordinate partner in the relationship. We are just recently birthing ourselves out of patriarchal cultures that have been defined with men as the leader and women being the follower. The shift that relationships are going through started in the 1960s with the women's liberation movement.

At the time, some of this cultural shift was seen as a negative change that could destroy the family unit. As a child of the 60s, I distinctly remember the backlash from the role of women changing in society. As is the case in most cultural shifts, people are not conscious enough to mentally embrace and work with the energetic shifts that are occurring, so their defense mechanisms are triggered. The collective limiting belief can play out that, "change is a threat." What we have seen instead of destruction is the rise of women to become partners with the men in their lives and men rising up to become partners with their wives in their role as parents.

In the new experience of partnership, wives and husbands have an opportunity to learn how to create the personal autonomy of two people who choose to come together in a committed union of partnership.

Partnership Is Key

Now that hierarchy in relationships is collapsing, we are left to create something different. The different pattern that is available to us is the experience of partnership. In an intimate relationship, this looks like two people coming together as equals to create an intimate experience together that helps us refine ourselves to become better people.

In a partner-themed relationship you will both feel you can speak what is true for you, be heard, share your most vulnerable selves, talk about difficult subjects and work things out. In a partner-themed relationship, you come together in your parenting efforts, both have a say, and are committed to the best outcome for your children. You are an open book when it comes to finances and both parties know the financial status of your couple-ship. You have a healthy and active sexual experience that first brings pleasure to each of you and secondarily is pleasurable to your partner. You talk about how the household is run, how the kids are being raised, the ways you want to spend your money, and what experiences you want to have together and separately. You are aware of each other's needs and wants and come together to work on supporting each other without being emotionally dependent on each other. Emotional support looks like buoying each other up when needed, giving emotional support without your partner being emotionally dependent on you to feel good about themselves.

This doesn't mean you work on everything in your life as a couple. It means you have communicated to see what needs to be a couple decision and what can be managed by one of the two of you. For example, I am good at making money and currently am the primary money source in our relationship. Jon's natural gifts make him a much better money manager. I know generally what's going on with our finances, but he manages the day-to-day details of that. This is a decision we have made together, communicating as partners to create an affluent relationship.

Get to Know Your True Nature

The first step in creating an affluent relationship is knowing yourself, independent of anyone else. If you do not know yourself, think for yourself, and feel your own feelings, you are vulnerable to being coerced or just going along with your partner, whether you know it or not. If you aren't tuned into what you think and feel about any given scenario, you may put your attention first on what your partner thinks and feels, and often not even consider yourself. You may choose to be agreeable just to avoid a conflict, while ignoring your wants and desires at a deeper level. If you want a true partner relationship, you need to show up as a full participant with feelings, desires, and needs that you know and value as much as anyone else's.

In a hierarchical relationship, one person runs the show and is the alpha energy of the relationship. When the energy of the culture supported this configuration, it worked fine. Many of us come from families where this was the energetic setup for our parents. My dad was the alpha. My mom just went along with him. She rarely considered what she wanted or expressed how she really felt about something. She catered heavily to my father and did not operate within their relationship as a self-realized woman. My dad was the guy in charge and my mom saw her role as catering to him. You may come from a family where this was the setup in your parents' relationship, or your mom was the alpha and dad just went along with her. Either way, these setups do not model how to create autonomy within a partnership. So this is new territory for most of us!

As those old relationship themes are falling apart, we are left to find ourselves and bring our true selves to our intimate relationship experience. This can take years to master, but every day, you are being given a chance to practice being your true self in your relationship.

It's common for women to default into the subordinate role with their partners. We have been conditioned strongly by modern-day love stories, songs, and princess tales that men are our knights in shining armor. Women are still waking up from the myth that male acceptance makes them more valuable. This is just old residue from past cultures when women had no rights or financial assets independent of a man. These old programs are unwinding within us, yet at times, women still want the knight in shining armor to save them, so they feel a pretense of value and importance. It is much more satisfying and permanent to first save yourself and see your own value and importance.

True to the process of creation, what we believe, we see. So, as you start to value yourself more, your partner will start showing up to share in that celebration of your truth and value. By giving yourself the validation, you'll also receive the validation that you once gave him the power to decide.

If you are still unconsciously or consciously looking to your partner for validation and permission to be yourself, take that power and decision back and do it for yourself. It was never your partner's job. It's always been yours. The part of you that has given the job to your spouse is your inner child who did not get enough approval and validation from your parents. Tell your inner child that you are their new, healthy parent and you are going to make up for what Mom and Dad fell short on. Use the "Fire Your Parents" visualization in this week's Practice to assist you in claiming your self-approval power back. Stop looking to your partner to validate you. Start giving yourself the validation you are seeking.

In the process of coming to know your true self better, I invite you to learn about your human nature in my body of work called Energy Profiling. As I've mentioned before, we are each born with an innate nature—the natural way that we move through life. This movement can be classified into one of four general expressions of human characteristics that I call the 4 Energy Types. Understanding your own Energy Type will assist you in having a greater clarity about who you are naturally designed to be so you can live true to who you are effortlessly.

As well as giving you a point of reference for your own natural gifts and tendencies, knowing your Energy Type will help you identify which of those gifts and tendencies were shamed in your childhood and are ready to be healed. If you have not healed the shaming references to your true self, you are most likely still trying to alter and change who you are, and you also may feel and even experience your partner judging and shaming who you are meant to be. This book does not have space to cover all 4 Energy Types, but I've created multiple resources to help you discover your Energy Type, including an online course and a book, which are free or affordable. You can find them listed in the appendix of this book.

As you set the intention to know your true self in your relationship, consider where you sell yourself short or compromise being true to yourself in your relationship. When you do that, notice how that leaves you feeling. It will bring up feelings of resentment, either focused on yourself or your partner. That's a good thing, as it's a message to you to do it differently. It can help you know where you need to practice maintaining autonomy in your intimate relationship.

What you believe about yourself, your
partner will reflect back to you.

Get to Know Your Partner's True Nature

Once you have insights on how to more fully live true to who you are, the next step is to more clearly understand your partner's natural gifts and tendencies. This will give you the advantage to no longer have false and unrealistic expectations, expecting them to be someone different. Most couple misunderstandings or contention are a result of two people not understanding each other, not respecting each other's differences, and then projecting false expectations on each other as a result.

When you remove misunderstandings caused by unreasonable expectations, you open the space to naturally have more harmony and cooperation. With enlightened understanding of each other, you and your partner have more realistic expectations, which naturally turns into more peace and love between you—the experience we all strive for in our close relationships.

After you learn about your Energy Type, make it a point to learn about your spouse or partner's Energy Type, so you can see them for who God designed them to be, honor their natural gifts and tendencies, and appreciate those character traits in them. Those expressive qualities originally attracted you to them!

Understanding each other's Energy Type was one of the biggest relationship game changers in my marriage. Jon and I have had a highly challenging relationship that has forced us to learn, change, and either grow or get divorced. We passed through many periods of time when we felt divorce may be the only answer to end the contention and pain we both felt within the experience of our relationship.

Jon and I were married in 1980. As baby boomers, we were the last generation to come from the traditional male/female hierarchy of relationships. We married with the understanding that he was to be the main provider and I would be the stay-at-home parent. He was meant to be the yang energy of the relationship and I was meant to be the yin energy of the relationship. The yang male was the cultural stereotype of the time: the go-getter, the guy in charge, the strong and aggressive man. The yin female was the cultural stereotype of the time: the submissive, soft and charming, sweet and sensitive woman.

Turns out, Jon and I were nothing like the stereotypical cultural references of the day. I got after him constantly for not being more of a self-starter, going after what he wanted, making more money and being the strong male in my life. He constantly got after me to be more sensitive and soft, to follow his lead and just trust him.

Then we learned our Energy Types. We learned Jon was the yin masculine and I was the yang feminine! Jon has a soft and sensitive nature, is not a natural go-getter, and is definitely not aggressive. He needs to plan things out, move forward in a methodical, step-by-step process, and stop to check in with how he feels along the way. I am the natural go-getter, the grab-the-bulls-by-the-horn kind of gal. It turns out, I am much more of an entrepreneur than he is and have a lot of confidence when it comes to creating a lot of money. We both naturally moved through the world in our own way, and no amount of pushing or hoping from the other would change our true natures.

Once we had these insights, we could stop the process of mis-judging and projecting false expectations on each other. It didn't happen overnight, and we still have to remind ourselves, yet this knowledge has dramatically opened our relationship to experi-ence more love and appreciation for each other and definitely a lot more harmony.

I have heard from thousands of couples that have shared with me similar stories as this one:

"Before I knew my husband's Energy Type, I wrongfully labeled him as lazy and unhelpful. And to my high-energy self, that seemed completely accurate! I'm doing 4 things in the span of 30 minutes while he's chilling on the couch.

Normally, I would hold in my resentment and then explode and then he would be upset and shut down and withdraw. I wondered how he could be so insensitive, while he wondered why I didn't just ask.

Tonight, on the other hand, I called him into the kitchen and asked for a hug. I asked him if he would put our daughter to bed tonight and explained how that would be supportive to me. I filled him in on what I was trying to get done and why, and he told me he would be happy to do that. In the past, I would have just resented the fact that he wasn't moving through life like me and getting more done. I now know I am the higher movement of the two of us, and when asked in a sensitive way, he is more than willing to step in and help me out."

I have had the pleasure of hearing from couples all over the world about the benefits of knowing each other's Energy Type, and in many cases how it has saved their marriage. Give yourself this advantage. Learn about Energy Profiling to discover your and your partner's Energy Types. This first step to understanding each other makes all the other steps easier. A commitment to embracing your strengths and recognizing your partner's strengths will support you in building a supportive partnership for you both.

We are learning the lessons of collaboration and partnership in our most intimate relationships and our families first. As we continue to do this, we will learn to extend these lessons to our societies.

Communication 101

Any great partnership involves great communication. Good communication skills that are used frequently become the bedrock of a partner-themed relationship.

Like many people, Jon and I dated and dated until we met the person who would perfectly push our buttons—and we got married! We did not know how to communicate. Neither of us came from families where we witnessed our parents using communication skills to get along, work together, and work things out. My mom modeled just going along with my dad and Jon's parents modeled that everything was always fine, no matter what. We had to learn communication skills on our own. I wasn't willing to play the role of the "Yes, dear" wife, and things were not always fine. We had issues, and those issues began to hijack our love for each other early in the relationship. Our most common expression of communication turned into arguing with each other.

If this scenario sounds familiar to you, rather than throw in the towel on your relationship, consider the possibility that you signed on to create new relationship patterns in your family system. As I look back, I can now see that Jon and I were in an uncharted relationship wilderness. We had come into our relationship at a time when the energy was shifting. Unbeknownst to us, we were forerunners in creating new relationship patterns within our family systems. Our children and grandchildren have been benefactors of our work and commitment to create a healthy partnership. Each of our married children were joined together in a partnership energy that we helped birth in our family, and their relationships have not had any of the struggles that Jon and I faced.

You could be a relationship pioneer in your family. If that is the case, you can be led by inspiration to create new relationship patterns. Stay the course. And learn healthy communication skills to help you create success!

If you want to learn how to communicate effectively in a partnership, you can find entire books written on the subject. I highly encourage you to study those you are drawn to. Jon and I studied resources that were correct for us to develop valuable communication skills and create an affluent relationship

Here is a synopsis of the most important takeaways that we have learned over the years:

1. When someone is emotionally charged, their brain is flooded with emotion and they cannot make rational decisions. As I mentioned above, we date and date until we meet the person who will push our emotional buttons more than anyone else and then we marry them. With that in mind, there will be many times when both partners are emotionally charged and cannot have a rational conversation. You need to both agree that when that is playing out, one of you says, "We are both emotionally flooded and we cannot have a civil conversation about this. Let's talk about it when we are both clear." Then the other person says, "Okay." You both agree to come back together at a mutually supportive time and talk about the presenting issue. Then you go to different rooms to

give you the energetic space to shift into a calmer state. If this happens while you are driving somewhere in the car, stop the car. One of you get in the back seat. Giving yourself your own personal space will allow the emotional energy to shift much faster and you won't be as vulnerable to take on each other's energy.

2. When you're talking about an emotionally charged topic, decide to take turns as the talker and the listener. The talker has the floor. The listener does not need to agree with what is being shared by the talker; their role is just to understand. This is called empathic listening—listening in order to understand the other's experience. You can set up a time limit for the talker role. We often do this and put our timer on the agreed-upon timeline so when the time is up, we switch roles. The key to being a good listener is to every few sentences, say back to the talker any of the following that fit:

   - *So, what you are sharing is...*
   - *How you feel about this is...*
   - *What you want is...*
   - *What really hurts you is...*

You are practicing reflective listening skills. Remember: no fixing, no lecturing, no advising, no taking your turn to share your stuff, just listening to understand.

After you have both felt heard and understood, you can each take a turn to share what you want and recommend action items that you can both agree on. Once people feel heard and understood, they are usually more agreeable to work together in coming up with a mutually agreeable solution. These steps work like magic for Jon and me. We have both learned that, more than getting our way, we just want to be heard. Once we are both heard, it's quite easy to come up with a solution together.

3. Recognize different styles of communication, for example:

   Chit-chat and talking shop is more surface-level communication that includes talking about schedules, to-do's, and happenings of the family. It is light conversation about everyday things.

   Hostile and control talk is a way of exerting your power by speaking for your partner, advising, prescribing solutions, criticizing in subtle or non-subtle ways, and putting down your partner's decisions or traits that you don't agree with or don't like.

   Inquiry talk is showing interest and engaging in a conversation that supports each partner in learning more about the other. It involves asking questions, learning from each other, honoring each other's opinions, identifying issues and brainstorming to come up with collaborative outcomes. (This is the communication style that is experienced if you apply tip #4 taught below.)

Awareness talk is the practice of staying mindful of your emotions and your partner's emotions, not letting them dictate your communication choices if you or your partner are triggered. It's seeing the bigger picture of what is really playing out, recognizing emotional triggers rooted in old childhood issues that are being mimicked in your relationship. It's the practice of one or both of you being mindful enough to step away temporarily or listen well. It's staying in your adult energy, no matter the emotion that is surfacing, and maintaining a civil interaction together.

Which style of communication do you practice most often in your relationship? A lot of couples get stuck in only doing chit-chat and hostile/control talk and never take time for the inquiry and awareness communication experiences. These last two styles are worth taking the time to practice.

4. Set up an official weekly talking time. Jon and I do this every Sunday at 2 p.m. We each get the floor for about 15-30 minutes as the talker, the other person just listens, and then we switch roles. In our weekly talking

times, we have a chance to share ourselves, what's on our minds, things we are excited about, things we are learning, things we want feedback on. It's an open and safe space to share. Since Jon's nature is more introverted, he is the one who felt the most unheard in our relationship. I suggested we set this up so that he had a regular space to share himself. At first, he felt vulnerable, as he had spent his entire life keeping things inside and not feeling he had a right or a space to be heard. It took some practice for him to feel comfortable sharing himself, especially his feelings. We both have benefitted greatly from this practice, as we both came from families where we were not encouraged to share ourselves.

5. Do not finish each other's sentences, talk over each other, or interrupt. Let the other person take the time they need to express themselves.

6. No matter what, choose to be civil with each other. This is important, as it creates a safe relationship environment. When we feel safe, we are more apt to share our feelings. Being civil includes using a civil tone of voice, never making the other person a brunt of a joke, and never using harsh humor that really just puts someone down as a joke. No teasing and most of all, no yelling or raising of your voice.

One of the best books I read recently is titled, *Choosing Civility—The Twenty-Five Rules of Considerate Conduct,*

By P.M. Forni.[xvi] With what appears to be a decreasing amount of thoughtful behavior and common decency in the world, it's become even more important to choose civility in our most intimate relationships. Our societies will only become more civil if each of us chooses civility in all spaces of our lives. We tend to show our worst behavior to those we love the most. Let's make sure to show our best behavior to those we love most.

7. Share with each other the one thing you really need and want the other person to do for you in the relationship. Here are ours:
Jon: Make physical contact with him on a daily basis. Jon was the middle child of seven children and he did not get one of his basic needs met as a child—being hugged and touched on a regular basis. This is supportive to him to know he is loved.

Carol: Be kind in word and actions, no matter what. I grew up in a family where a lot of teasing and harsh humor was practiced. Having all brothers and a very domineering, abusive father, I was not the recipient of kindness on a routine basis. This is supportive to me to know I am safe in a relationship.

I believe the number one priority to work on if you want to experience an affluent relationship is communication. In marriage, collaboration involves a strong man and a strong woman who can come together to create an experience of partnership where the whole is greater than the sum of its parts. It is guaranteed you will have challenges in your relationship. Collaboration does not come naturally; it is created by learning and using healthy communication skills.

"If we are kind and considerate, people will want to be around us, and we benefit from enduring circles of attention and care." —*P.M. Forni*

Intimacy Evolved

My husband's and my intimate and sexual experience was broken from the go! We both had to work through several layers of wounding over several decades to get to the place where we are now of an honoring and enjoyable sexual experience. If you are experiencing sexual dysfunction in your relationship, my hope is that you will move through the healing process much faster than we did to reap the joyful benefits of a successful intimate and sexual experience together.

My own wounding came from years of sexual abuse in childhood. It was also complicated by old religious programming that suggested that sex is a sin. With years of dedicated effort on my part, I can happily say I have healed and claimed my sexual energy and now truly enjoy a regular sexual experience where the pleasures of that experience are for me first. Here are my top five tips to help you find, heal, and claim your sexual energy so it blesses your life:

1. Make sure that sex is for you first. If you have a background of abuse, you would have learned that sex was for the pleasure of the person subjecting you to the sexual acts you were forced to participate in. Even if you were not sexually abused, you may have been abused by the media's misrepresentation of a woman's sexuality being an expression to first please and pleasure a man.

   When you are forced to feel the sexual functions in your body in your childhood, premature and out of context of a loving relationship, sexual sensations in your body feel like a threat and are very frightening psychologically, emotionally and may even feel like death to your body. Your sex drive is hampered and repressed as those feelings are not comfortable, and sexual activities can trigger the feeling that you are being abused all over again. Even orgasm, which is a natural function, can be hampered. If you orgasmed as a child or teen in the event of abuse, your body may be resistant to it when it is now appropriate and desired.

   What was critical for me in learning that my sexual experience existed for my own pleasure first, was to engage in the act of pleasuring myself without my husband participating. When you feel your body and your sexuality were taken from you at an early age, self-pleasure can become an act of taking your body and sexuality back. I had to claim back my own body and all of its sensations, many that I had never even felt before I chose to do this. Achieving sexual climax on my own without the involvement of my husband was one of the most freeing moments of my sexual healing. I reclaimed myself on all levels. Being able to work through layers of discomfort by myself, without feeling the pressure of my husband's experience, was a healing practice which made our partner sex more erotic and pleasurable for both of us.

How can you do this? There are plenty of sex toys on the market to help you with this healing process. Find a Pure Romance consultant in your area, as they provide resources, education, and safe home-party environments to learn and invest in what they offer. I also encourage you to work with a professionally trained therapist, as I did that taught me how to move through this healing process to allow successful outcomes.

Our sexual energy is one of the most powerful energies we have available to us. I am grateful to have it now contribute to my and my husband's pleasure in our sexual experience together.

2. Send away the wounded little girl and get present in your adult body. We all carry generational patterns about sex, or we experienced uncomfortable scenarios or conversations about sexuality when we were younger. If you experienced sexual abuse, it's incredibly common to recreate the same psychological and emotional state that you had to experience as a child when you are having sex as an adult. My trick for this was to take a few minutes before I engaged in sex with my husband and do a quick

visualization with my wounded inner child. I would meet
with her and tell her I was the adult having an adult
sexual experience I had chosen. I would invite her to go
away and play, bringing in angels to help her and remove
her from the scene. I told her she was not the one having
sex. I was, as the adult. This helped me stay present and
create new patterns of thought and feelings that were
positive about having sex.

3. Talk about your fears and get them out of your body.
   My husband proved to be a good listener for me when
   I needed to do this. I encouraged him that he didn't
   need to fix anything, that it was therapeutic for me
   to just be able to put to words what I was feeling so
   I wouldn't store it in my body. If your spouse is not
   able to support you in this way, it is worth it to pay
   a counselor to have a space to share what you have
   never put words to. Feelings need a form of expression, and having your body overcome with anger and
   fear at the time of having sex will not allow you to stay
   present enough to teach your body that sex is meant to
   be a pleasurable experience.

4. Work with a great sex therapist.
   Jon and I had the privilege of working with a wonderful sex therapist who helped me clean up some final
   stages of my healing and actually helped Jon heal
   some of his own sexual wounding.

5. Learn how your body's sexual biology functions.

   Do you know the name and function of all of your sexual and reproductive organs? I didn't. That is why I read the book, *Anatomy of Arousal* by Sheri Winston.[xvii] Again, in an effort to claim my body back for myself first, and to create a healthy relationship with my body, I learned about how it works and what it is designed to do sexually which was supportive.

Since my sexual wounding took center stage in our intimate relationships for many years, it wasn't until we met with a sex therapist several years ago that we realized my husband had some sexual baggage of his own to deal with. My husband's wounding came primarily from religious programming that sex was bad. In an effort to maintain his morality as a youth, he was taught that sex was forbidden before marriage, and that any form of contact with his own body was a vile sin. Your values are not the issue here—whether you align with the value of no sex before marriage or not—what is important is how that value was handled. If values surrounding sex were handled in a shaming way as you were growing up, then your sexuality was wounded.

In my husband's case, his sexual energy and bodily functions were shamed and never talked about in a positive and educational way during his youth. He was left to feel that shame, with no support from his parents to dialogue about his developing body in a healthy way that would teach him to love, honor, and work with it. As an adult, Jon was left to re-parent his teenage self and help grow up that part of himself from the shame energy he had been left to exist in. He had to teach that part of himself that it is natural for a male to have ejaculations in his youth and that he needs to learn about his biology to consciously support his body and his sexuality.

He also had to teach that part of himself that it was not his wife's job to provide sexual fulfillment for him. All through his youth, he had been given messages that his sexual fantasies would be fulfilled once he was married. This left him subconsciously believing that it would be his wife's job to play out the function of fulfilling them. Our honeymoon night was a disaster! He was hot to trot and I was scared and shut down! It began a pattern of anger and frustration for both of us that lasted for years. The expectation he projected that it was my job to fulfill his sexual desires constantly triggered my feelings of being victimized and used only for sex. And my resistance then triggered his shame and guilt for wanting something that was labeled "bad."

Anger was the common emotional response for us, but not at the time of the issue. It would just be played out in day-to-day interactions. True to our nature, my yang energy expressed anger in a loud, volatile, outward manner, and his yin energy expressed anger by shutting down and going away, which I perceived as abandonment. The same scenes would play out over and over again. After 20 years of this, we finally could see that we were like a broken record. We even said we should just record the next argument and play it instead of wasting the energy to act it out again. We both blamed each other insistently for years. We both had no clue that we were dealing with so much pent up anger that was driven from pent up sexual energy that had no healthy expression.

We came from generations that lacked healthy sexual teachings in our homes. My mom had the 15-minute chat with me and it must not have been shared in a positive way, as she claims my response was, "I have to do that?" My husband's father pulled him aside the night before we were married to basically give him a quick heads up to make sure he knew what was happening. Taking the time to learn more as adults was supportive to us. Along with working with a sex therapist, which served my husband and I beautifully in both claiming back our sexual selves, another great resource we invested in was working with a sex coach.

You may be asking, what is a sex coach? For us, it was a gentleman who was not a therapist, but someone who knew a lot about sex and how to create a great sexual partnership. He gave us activities to participate in, videos to study and learn from, and coaching on how to have a more interesting and exciting sexual experience together. We both felt the need to invest in this, as we had seen the sexual experience of our relationship start at the bottom of the barrel. We were both committed and having fun making it a healthy part of our affluent relationship.

It took Jon and I years to peel the onion of what we were taught and the shaming we both experienced around sex, mostly because we ignored it for many of the early years and did not have the communication skills to even begin working through it. When we were finally ready, we peeled the onion in the context of a committed partnership, which supported us both. Where the conversations used to be hard and awkward about our sexual experience, they are now open, interesting, and supportive.

A healthy sexual experience is a big player in experiencing affluence in your relationship. It's connected to all other aspects of your relationship, such as communication and the strength of your partnership. What needs to be addressed in your sexual experience so it can contribute to the affluence of your overall relationship?

Become the "Eve" of Your Relationship

Creating an affluent relationship can be more challenging to achieve results in as quickly as you experience in the other five lessons. This is due to the fact it takes both you and a partner being committed to personal changes in yourself and how you relate to each other to practice over years. Yet, you can see some immediate positive changes when both partners are willing to commit to making changes. But what do you do if you have a partner who is not interested in this opportunity?

First, do not just assume they are not interested. I see a pattern of women being the early adopters when it comes to doing this kind of spiritual, personal, and relationship work. Why is that? Is it possible that our brains are wired to be more aware of spiritual and emotional experiences and we see the potential that we are not yet experiencing?

There's a pattern that could have been established in the biblical story of the original couple, Adam and Eve. In simple terms, Adam and Eve lived in the Garden of Eden, where God told them not to eat the fruit of the knowledge of good and evil. Lucifer came and tempted Adam first to counter God's command and eat the fruit. He chose not to. So Lucifer went to Eve and gave her the same temptation to eat the fruit. She knew that it would cause her to be cast out of the garden without Adam joining her. At the moment of her decision, Eve thought for herself. She did not say, "Wait a minute, Lucifer, I have to go consult with Adam to see what he wants to do," and then base her decision on Adam's opinion. She made a choice independent of Adam and then went and shared with him what she had chosen. This ultimately influenced his decision to follow her lead.

Could it be that the feminine leading the masculine in spiritual and personal growth is a pattern set in place by Eve, in order to realize its full potential at a time when feminine energy is returning to the planet in full balance with the masculine? Are we being called to play this role? I'd like to think so. When it comes to your spiritual, personal, and relationship growth, consider the possibility that you are the leader in this part of your relationship. Rather than just conclude, "He's not interested, he would never do any of this." Assume that he's just waiting for you to pave the way and lead you both into more affluence in your relationship and all areas of your life.

Where in your life are you being asked to be the "Eve?" Trust that you will be led and guided in how to influence your partner in a way that they also chose to seek something better for themselves and your relationship. Often, it just means you need to bring it up and be willing to talk about your desires and what you want in the relationship.

I could write an entire book on relationships. For now, I trust you have gained useful insights from the teachings in this lesson, the Clear, Activate, and Practice portions of this lesson will help you move forward in the process of creating an affluent relationship.

Tips for Raising Relationally Affluent Children

What are you modeling for your children about how to relate to a partner? This is an area of life where actions speak much louder than words. If you want your children to learn how to create an affluent relationship, practice it yourself and show them.

Along with being a healthy role model for your children, you can teach your children effective communication skills that will serve them in a multitude of ways in their life. Not only will they have skills for their intimate relationship, good communication will serve them in all relationships, along with professional activities.

Once you establish more effective communication skills, start to teach them to your children. They will have a chance to use them with you and their siblings. Rather than try and teach these skills in the moment they are most needed, set up a couple of times a month to gather as a family and learn about communication skills. Incentivize your children with a family activity or reward by tracking your success. If one child needs more support in this area, take them aside and do it privately. Let them know you want to help them feel heard and understood, so you want to teach them some methods to be able to achieve that.

Take each of your children aside and in a dedicated one-on-one time, ask them the following questions:

- *Do you feel heard and understood in our family?*
- *Is there anything you're not sharing because you are afraid it will be made fun of?*
- *Is there anything you are keeping to yourself because you are afraid it will get you in trouble?*
- *Is there anything you want to tell me or talk about?*

Just listen to your child's answers. Choose not to advise, lecture, fix, or give your opinion on what they are sharing. You want to establish trust that you can listen because your primary motive is to understand them. Once your children feel heard and understood, they will be more open to hear your feedback at a later time in a different setting, and they can practice listening to understand when you share.

With good communication skills, you build a trusting and loving relationship with your child. This is a strong benefit when it comes to teaching them about their sexuality and how to manage this powerful energy in a way that is honoring of them and to others. It is a parent's sacred right to be the lead in teaching and training a child how to embrace their sexual expressive self. Two places where parents may give up this right are in educational or religious settings. Make sure you take the lead as a parent to influence what information your child is receiving and what messages they hear from you. Let educational or religious leaders know your boundaries and request that they always include you first to inquire if you are comfortable with your child learning or having certain conversations. It's your right as their parent to do what is in the best interest of your child so they can grow up with a healthy sexual esteem.

Another great tool to teach your child how to create an affluent life is the tool of their imagination. Start with teaching them how to use it to create affluence during their childhood, right in their own family experience. To help teach your children how to use their imagination to create an affluent family experience, at a family gathering play the "What if our family could..." game. Just have everyone close their eyes and do the following easy visualization. Say to your children:

- *What if our family could be like this, what would you like to experience more of in our family? Imagine...*
- *Everyone getting along in our family.*
- *You become best friends with the sibling you are fighting with a lot.*
- *You are best buds.*
- *You feel heard and understood by Mom and Dad.*
- *We are all having fun together doing...*
- *We have enough money and to spare and use it for our highest good as a family.*
- *What do you want to experience in our family? Take a minute and imagine it.*

After this short visualization, invite your family members to share what they were imagining. Set the ground rule that no one can mock, make fun, tease each other, or criticize what is being shared. Teach your children that creating affluence starts with their imagination—the mental energy field. Then celebrate the potential your family has by expressing positive uplifting emotion with each other. Honor how different family members do that. (As you can learn in the Energy Profiling system, some Energy Types have a higher, more expressive energy, while other Energy Types are more calm and serious in their expressive selves. It's all good.)

When you manifest your imagined outcomes, make sure to note them as family and celebrate the affluence you are creating together.

Relationship Affluence Step 1: CLEAR

Repeat the following clearing script out loud to clear and release your old relationship beliefs and patterns of lack, pain and struggle:

It is time and I am ready to release and clear any and all patterns that keep me creating struggle and hardship in my relationships.

I choose to own the truth that I am the origin of all struggle that I experience in any relationship, as I am the one experiencing it.

I let go of family relationship patterns that have set me up to make relationships hard and painful.

I release all beliefs, both conscious and unconscious, that contribute to not being heard in my relationships, any need to control so I can attempt to be heard, all perceptions of blame that it is the other person's fault that this relationship is hard.

I let go of all compromises I make and fears of not speaking up, being vulnerable and being my true self in the relationship.

I release all emotional attachments to my partner, and the belief that it is their job to make me feel good about myself.

I release any known and unknown beliefs, perceptions, assumptions, emotions, family patterns, blind spots, habits, and anything else that is keeping my relationship in a compromised state.

Relationship Affluence Step 2: ACTIVATE

Repeat the following activation script out loud to help create relationship patterns of affluence, ease, and joy:

I now activate my full potential to experience a partnership where both partners feel loved, heard, understood, and supported.

I understand that creating an affluent relationship starts with me and getting to know my own true nature, which I now choose.

I am also knowing and understanding my partner's true nature.

I am amazed at how willing my partner is in actively joining me in this same practice.

Every part of our relationship improves as we understand ourselves and each other more clearly.

Talking and communication comes easily to us.

It's amazing how well we work things out together.

We have an active and rewarding sexual experience together.

We consistently model to our children how to create affluence and partnership in a marriage.

I am experiencing an affluent relationship of harmony and collaboration that is a joy to my life.

Relationship Affluence Step 3: PRACTICE

For one week, do the following activities to help you create a strong foundation for your affluent relationship.

1. Your mantra for this lesson is: *I am experiencing a harmonious and collaborative partnership with my partner.* Using a dry erase marker, write this mantra on your bathroom mirror and repeat it every morning.

2. Read the Clear and Activate scripts for relationship affluence each day in the morning.

3. Fire Your Parents Visualization
   In a marriage, it is common to unconsciously assign your spouse to play out similar roles that your parents played for you. You then tend to look to your spouse as the substitute parent to try and get them to meet any unmet emotional needs you still have outstanding. This short visualization will shift the energy away from your parents and your spouse having to take care of your inner child. It moves that responsibility to yourself, as you are the most capable of taking care of your emotional self as the evolving adult. If you find it helpful, you can record this visualization and listen to it.

Imagine yourself in the light with God and the angels. Feel the love that is there for you. Imagine a timeline that takes you back into your past. You move along the timeline with the support of your angels as you are taken back to a home in your childhood. You feel safe and secure to enter the home and invite your inner child to come to you. If this child is hesitant, let them know who you are: I am your adult self, I am here to help you. If your child self has had repeated negative experiences with adults, this part of you may be hesitant. Tell your child self that it's okay, you understand, they can take the time they need to develop trust. If your child self is excited to see you, go to them, bend down on your knees and give them a hug and let them know how much you love them and care for them and that you came to help them. With your child self standing by your side, invite your mom and dad to come forward. Thank them for playing the role of your parents, that you trust they did the best they knew how, considering their history and story they probably still live by. Let them know you have come to take over the job of parenting your younger self and you are choosing to fire them from being the caregiver of your emotional needs. You have learned that you are the best one to help grow yourself up emotionally. In fact, you want to help them choose the same so you called in their angels to come and get them and take them to a place of healing where they can get the emotional help they need. Thank them again and see them depart with their angels. Turn to your child self and let them know you are there for them and you want to help them. You see your spouse close by, waving to you. You point to your spouse and share with your inner child: That person is not your parent either; I no longer want you to turn to my spouse to try and get your emotional needs met. Let them know it never works out and it will only let them down or make them angry that your spouse is not showing up the way your child self wants them to! Again, reassure this part of yourself that you are the one to help them with their emotional needs. Embrace your inner child and bring them into your heart to reside within you in a loving place. Take a deep breath in and let the energy grow up inside of you.

This is a powerful visualization and is not a one-and-done process. Any time you are emotionally triggered by your spouse or are running your "needy child" energy with them, take a moment and do this visualization to release your parents and spouse from a role that will never help you grow up emotionally.

4. Set up a Talking Time with Your Spouse.
   Each of you take turns answering any of the following questions (or others you decide you want to ask). Just listen and learn from each other. In order to start talking about more difficult issues, trust needs to be built. Trust is built when people know they are heard and understood. The goal of this talking time is for both people to have the experience of being heard and understood—not to work on any issues. If you sense any of these questions could turn into a fight or need to do more personal emotional work before you're ready to hear the answers, avoid them.

- *Are you happy with the amount of time we spend together?*
- *Name your least favorite household chore.*
- *How could I be a better wife/husband?*
- *What hobby would you like to take up together?*
- *What is one thing you discovered about yourself this week?*
- *In what areas is it hardest to be "totally" open and honest with me?*
- *How can I be a better mother/father?*
- *What is one aspect in your parents' relationship that you would like to mimic in ours?*
- *What is one pattern in your parents' relationship that would like to make sure we choose not to re-create?*
- *Are you content or satisfied with the way your life is right now?*
- *What's one thing I have never done for you that you wish I would? (With the exception of sexual activities.)*
- *What is your favorite meal as of today?*
- *How did we make each other smile this week?*
- *What things do I do for you that you absolutely don't want me to stop?*
- *Were there any actions or words I expressed toward you this week that were hurtful to you?*
- *If we had a theme song, what would it be?*
- *What's your favorite place we've visited?*
- *When have you needed me to take initiative but I didn't?*
- *How are we different?*
- *How are we similar?*
- *What do I do that sends you the message I really love you?*

- *What is one thing I can do more of that sends you the message that I love you?*
- *Is there anything you have never told me?*
- *What supports you in experiencing more joy?*
- *What desires do you have that you would like more support with?*

5. What other areas can you give attention to this week? Choose one of the following areas of your life and invest the time and money to start working on it to directly support an affluent relationship:

   A. *Learn about your true nature in my Energy Profiling system.*
   B. *Learn about your spouse's true nature in my Energy Profiling System.*
   C. *Take the next step in healing any sexual wounding by investing in therapy, books, or any other resources you are guided to seek out to support you. What is your next correct step in healing any old sexual wounding?*

6. What insights did you learn in Lesson 6 that you want to implement in to your relationship? What action steps can you take this week to start implementing it?

7. For additional support this week please use any of the Relationship Clearing Scripts found in the appendix.

Insights from Lesson 6

Where Do I Go From Here?

Now that you have completed the six-week practice, take time to let the energy settle and integrate. You have done more inner and outer work in the last six weeks than possibly ever in your life. Congratulations!

I recommend you do the six-week lesson experience as many times as you feel moved to. Take at least two weeks between sessions to allow the energy to integrate and settle. How many times do you need to do this? As many times as it serves you. Just make sure that you do not get in the habit and mindset that you still "need" healing. At the end of a six-week practice, you are an entirely different person. You have achieved a higher state of awareness of yourself and your life.

After finishing a six-week practice, your life may not appear that much different to you or others in the bigger picture of how everything is playing out. But in the little nuances of your day-to-day experience, you will experience dramatic changes. Over time, the bigger stage of your life will all take on an experience of affluence. You may experience a dramatic change in your spirituality, your mental and emotional health, you may experience healing of diseases or ailments that have been long-standing patterns, you may have a dramatic increase in your financial flow and accumulation, and you may enjoy a complete change for the better in your relationships. As I shared in the first part of the book, I have been practicing the process of mastering affluence on a daily basis for the last 15 years, and I continue to experience positive changes in all six areas of practice.

Now that you have finished the full six-week practice, you may also revisit sections of the book as you are drawn to them. The more you tune into the next correct step for you, the more you will experience affluence in all areas of your life.

As you start to experience more moments of sustained affluence and happiness for no apparent reason, you may think, "I'm there! I've got this!" Be aware that you may feel as if you have arrived and affluence will be a constant in your inner and outer world, only to then experience what feels like a setback or regression in the progress you have made. Expect moments like these, where you feel you are back in the energy of lack again. You are not back at the beginning. You are just receiving a message that there is more to clear and shift. In these six weeks, you have committed to long-term change, rather than short-term fixes. God and your soul are guiding you on this journey. Pay attention to the guidance and just let yourself feel the disappointment and frustration that may come up with what appears and feels like a setback. Note that those are the feelings of your inner child. You need to attend to that part of you that legitimately had no power to change their life and experienced disappointments far too often. The emotions are information for you to do more emotional healing.

The one thing I can tell you for sure is that we are not on a linear upward progression when it comes to changing our inner and outer world states from struggle to affluence. The progress is more like a wave pattern, an up and down. But there is a steady progression of up in the longer tracking of the pattern.

I would tell myself repeatedly, "I am in this for the long haul. I am pretty much doing everything I am striving to do differently to shift from struggle to affluence. I have thoughts every day, I have feelings every day, I am interacting with money every day, I am in a relationship every day of my life, I wake up in my body every day, and I have a spiritual practice I engage in every day." The changes happened for me by just deciding every day to do what I was already doing a little bit differently, because I trusted that in at least 20 years, I would for sure see positive change. Fortunately, it hasn't taken the full 20 years to see major changes and shifts.

When you have that experience of "happy for no reason" and then you hit a "struggle slump," be kind to yourself. You will notice that patterns you used to unconsciously live in every moment of your life, you are now conscious of, and that each time you move through the pattern, the process gets shorter and shorter. Jon and I started to point out to each other when we would slip into old relationship patterns of struggle. After we came out of it, one of us would acknowledge, "That only took three hours to move through! We used to live in that pattern and energy every day! We are getting faster at this!"

This up and down experience is normal, due to the fact it takes time to shift our lives! You'll learn the lessons of affluence in one area of your life, then you get to learn it all over again in another area. But that is why we are here. It is the new lesson of our time and you are the inspired student, called to learn the

319

lessons of affluence and help shift the energy for the generations that follow you.

Tammy, an online student, shared the following:

"I have been on an emotional and physical shutdown for several weeks. I feel this work working, but I also feel like some part of me does not want to feel better. I have a few days that I feel pretty good, and then suddenly I'm sick or so exhausted I'm in shutdown again."

If you relate to Tammy's experience, continue to remind yourself, "I don't have to live in that energy anymore." You might have to remind yourself every day for a period of time, because even though it is uncomfortable and you are now spiritually and mentally awake to know better, the old energy is what you have known for most of your life. Choose to not get mad at yourself! Be patient, you are on your way and there is no going back.

So, what is the answer to, "Where do I go from here?"

Wherever your soul takes you. This book is a tool designed to be a reference and resource for a long-term practice of mastering affluence. Each time you go through the six lessons, you will gain new awareness and new skills, both the principles and practice of how to create an affluent life. I trust that you are well on your way.

Trust yourself and trust that your journey is perfectly playing out for you. You live at a special time with a choice to create a life you love more than any other generation that has walked this earth. Believe that it can be manifest within your lifetime. Believe that you are setting into motion the potential for affluence far beyond what you can even imagine is possible for your posterity. Whether others recognize it or not, you are a gift to all of humanity, as your contribution to create beyond the norm of the current patterns of struggle is affecting all of humanity. I recognize your contribution and I thank you. Because of your work and dedication to wanting something more for yourself, my life and all others are blessed because of you.

God Bless You,
Carol Tuttle

Appendix 1

How Will These Clearing Scripts Help You?

You are constantly transmitting an energy into the field of consciousness, which then creates your personal reality. Your subconscious mind is one of the biggest players in influencing the quality of the energy you offer. How do you know what your subconscious mind still believes? Look at the feedback you are getting in what is showing up for you day to day. Clearing scripts support you in recognizing, stating, and clearing away the energy that no longer serves you, and creating space to allow new patterns of affluence.

I have personally used clearing scripts for over two decades. Years ago, I made a choice to be open to the feedback life was giving me. Rather than react to it, I chose to accept it and change it. Even after I made my decision, I still reacted sometimes and wanted to blame someone or something outside of myself for what was happening. Yet, I would always come back to the fact that I was the most powerful influencer in the equation of why and how life unfolded for me.

The more I recommitted to owning my life, choosing to look at my life as a mirror, recognizing that I still held beliefs and perceptions in my subconscious mind, and clearing them, the more my life changed for the better. Clearing scripts were key in that process.

The collection of clearing scripts I have put together for you represent some of the most universal beliefs still held in most people's conscious or subconscious mind. These beliefs cause people to create experiences of lack, pain, and struggle.

The first half of each script includes clearing and releasing statements that are designed to trigger and release any blocks to creating more affluence in your life. The wording is designed to accommodate many belief systems and to release various types of traumatic programming. Add your own words where you feel guided. The second half of each clearing script includes reframing statements, written like affirmations, designed to activate beliefs and emotions that you hold in your natural design as a being created for affluence.

Clearing and reframing your conscious and subconscious energetic patterns will free you up to create new lifestyle habits that are taught in the Practice section of each of the 6 Lessons. Since our lifestyle habits are well conditioned in us, we can sabotage the clearings we do if we do not commit to changing our life skills. Dramatic and lasting change occurs with the combination of clearing energy in our inner world, and changing our life skills in our outer world experience.

10 Important Tips on How to Use the Clearing Scripts

1. Read through each of the clearing scripts, one a day, during the week of the lesson you are currently focused on. There are six sections of the clearing scripts that coincide with the six lessons.

2. IMPORTANT: It is important when using a clearing script to complete the entire script. The scripts are divided into two parts. The first part involves the triggering of old beliefs and programs, using words and phrases that open the energy to allow a shift to occur. The second part includes the reframes and affirmations to activate the truth of new beliefs and programs that allow you to create new patterns of living. If you only do the first part, you are opening an energy that may leave you hanging out in a state of trauma. Do *both* parts of the clearing to complete the energy circuit of releasing and reframing to reset your system. If you do not have much time, just shorten both parts to accommodate the time you have.

3. If you only have time to do a portion of the clearing, I recommend you use the reframes in the script you are choosing to work with.

4. You may find that focusing on just the positive, the reframes, serves you better and allows a greater shift.

Try it and see how you feel. Trust yourself. You can also go back and forth between using the entire script and using only the reframe portion of the script.

5. Add your own wording when you feel prompted to do so.

6. When you are emotionally charged or triggered, you are dealing with a "presenting issue." This is a great time to use a clearing script that corresponds with what you are dealing with, thinking, and feeling. Remember, you are being "set up" to clear what is upsetting you. Go with it and use the script to move the energy from lack and struggle to affluence and joy.

7. Record your favorite scripts on a voice recording app on your phone or other device and listen to 2-3 clearing scripts a week. You can listen to them even while you are doing chores and odd jobs. Your subconscious mind is the part of you that holds most of your limiting beliefs so it is not necessary that you are consciously focused on the clearing script you are listening to.

8. Use the clearing scripts while practicing a healing modality. Some of the most common modalities that these scripts can be adapted to are EFT, Tapping, NLP, and Rapid Eye Therapy.

9. Use scripts on behalf of loved ones as a "Proxy Clearing."
   You can help a loved one, or even a friend, shift their
   energy when they are stuck in a place of lack and limitation by using the clearing script in their behalf. Just
   imagine that you are the other person and do the clearing script as if they are doing it. You cannot choose
   healing for others, but you can have a profound effect
   on shifting energy so that it opens the space for them
   to choose it for themselves. We are all connected in
   the field of consciousness and your clearing session on
   behalf of someone else is a great gift to give them. I
   have assisted hundreds of clients in proxy clearings and
   seen profound things change for the people they are
   doing them for. Patricia's story is just one of hundreds of
   examples of how powerful proxy clearing can be:

*"I did a proxy clearing for my mother and brother the morning of
a family party. Historically, family parties have been the place
where we have experienced conflict and tension and I leave
feeling dishonored and not heard—mimicking how I felt as a
child growing up. Later that day we all attended the party and
every one of us got along beautifully. It was a MIRACLE! I knew
it would work, I was just amazed at how fast and powerful it
was. It was such a pleasure to experience how everyone was more
lovable and peaceful so naturally. Thank you so much, Carol."*

10. If you are a healing practitioner or counselor who prac-
    tices any kind of healing modality, such as EFT, Tapping,
    NLP, Rapid Eye Therapy, or even massage therapy,
    you can use these scripts in your sessions. For massage
    therapists, you could play the clearing script, with your
    client's approval, while you are performing the massage.
    We can experience a lot of stuck and stored energy in our
    body system, and listening to a clearing script during a
    massage can help release this repressed energy. If you
    are a massage client you could listen to the recordings
    of a clearing script using a headset while you are getting
    your massage.

What are some other creative ways you could use these clearing scripts? As the ideas come, make note of them here.

SPIRITUAL CLEARING SCRIPTS

Clearing for Giving Your Spiritual Authority Away

This clearing script will assist you in clearing any conscious or subconscious beliefs that cause you to perceive your spiritual authority is outside of you, or any trapped emotional trauma in the genetic emotional history of your family. You may not have held the beliefs or had the experiences that the script represents, yet it is a strong possibility that one of your ancestors did and you still may be the carrier of the energy pattern.

Releasing and clearing all the times I let others be my spiritual authority. Letting go of...

- *The answers are outside of me*
- *I don't know what is correct for me*
- *Others know better than me*
- *I am afraid to know for myself*
- *It's too much responsibility to know for myself*
- *Do I have a right to follow my own spiritual path?*
- *How do I know when I get answers?*
- *Who do I trust?*
- *What's right, what's wrong? Confused*

Let it all go, from all parts of my being, releasing it from all generations that preceded me...

- *If I don't believe a certain way, I am going to be rejected by my family*

- *Angry at my parents, angry at religious leaders, angry at God*
- *Sabotaging myself by not trusting and following my own inner knowing*
- *Still looking for permission and approval from authority figures*
- *Don't trust myself, afraid to take responsibility*
- *Giving my power away, then resenting them*
- *Forced to do things by recipe or root*
- *Refusing to follow authority figures since I was forced to as a child*
- *Who am I to be my own spiritual authority? I'd rather do what others tell me to do*

Let it go, release these beliefs and perceptions once and for all Letting go of...

- *Don't know what to believe*
- *There is so much chaos in the world, the world is such an evil place*
- *Have to protect myself, have to make sure nothing bad happens to me and my family*
- *There is evil everywhere, have to watch my back*
- *The news of the day scares me, so many threats to survive*
- *Troubled, worried, I have no right to be joyful when the world is falling apart*
- *There are no more boundaries, right and wrong have gone out the window, no guidelines, anything goes*
- *Release fear from every cell in the body on all layers and levels of my being.*
- **Take 3 deep breaths and let it all go once and for all.**

Reframes
- *Imagine yourself standing in the light with your higher power, God, Christ, Angels, or your own Soul.*
- *Take a deep breath and recite the following:*
- *Thank you God I am endowed with my own spiritual compass*
- *I am following my own spiritual authority center*
- *I am inspired by divine sources*
- *The guidance I need comes from the divine and as I tune into it within myself, I am clear on what is correct for me*
- *I am moving forward in confidence*
- *I am in touch with my divine light*
- *I call on my inner guidance at all times*
- *I am accepting my spiritual birthright from God*

Making these connections with truth on all levels and layers of my being:
- *I am reclaiming my spiritual power*
- *I trust and listen to myself*
- *Since I am my own spiritual authority, I can choose to be guided by religious leaders that I trust to help guide me in life*
- *My spiritual instincts are good and strong*
- *I see and feel clarity in my spiritual self*
- *I listen to the Divine and I am guided*
- *I act with confidence and decisiveness about what is correct for me*
- *I am one with the Divine*

Making connections with truth on all levels, opening to the truth that resides in me:

- *I am perfect just as God created me*
- *The world is as safe as I believe it is*
- *The spirit guides me in making correct choices so my family and I are safe at all times*
- *I attract the good of the world into my reality*
- *I am excited about my new spiritual perspective*
- *Thank you God, I am safe, I am watched over, I am protected, I am at peace*
- *Take a deep breath while imagining filling your whole body full of light and truth. Do it two more times. Tap with both hands, using your fingertips, just below both collarbones 5-6 times. Tap on the top of your head while walking in place with a heavier stomp to ground the new energy you have activated into your body.*

Clearing for Old Religious Shaming

This will assist you in clearing any references you may have consciously or subconsciously taken on throughout your life that you are unworthy in God's eyes. If religious beliefs were ever used to manipulate, control, or cause you to feel that you are unworthy and unvalued as a human being, this script will also assist you in clearing that. This will include the belief that you must sacrifice and suffer to be a worthy person in God's eyes.

Releasing and letting go of all the lies and illusions I may be carrying including...

- *In order to have good will in God's eyes, I must sacrifice and go without. That's the spiritual thing to do.*
- *I must deny pleasure. The pleasure of enjoying food, my sexuality, good health and wellbeing, and amazing living spaces and environments.*
- *I am never good enough*
- *I am an unworthy person*
- *I can never do it right*
- *Wrong, bad, evil*
- ***Letting it all go once and for all...***
- *It's more spiritual to go without*
- *If I don't do this, God will reject me*
- *If I do this, God will reject me*
- *Feel immoral, unclean, unworthy*
- *I can never be forgiven for some of my choices, still punishing myself*
- *Guilty, shame, God won't answer my prayers*

- *Bad person, God thinks I am a bad person*
- *Bad things happen to bad people, don't expect it to get any better, I don't deserve it*
- *Life needs to be hard to make up for all the mistakes I've made in my life*
- *I don't deserve affluence, I am a bad person*

Releasing all the lies I may have heard from others. Letting go of all the lies I carry either consciously or subconsciously. Releasing...

- *Life needs to be hard in order for me to grow spiritually*
- *Scared of God, projecting a negative male authority figure image on to God*
- *Afraid of being found out, putting up an image, if people really knew me they wouldn't like me*
- ***Letting go of...***
- *Feeling immoral, unclean, unworthy, sinful*
- *It's not spiritual to have comfort and affluence*
- *Have to work and struggle to be good enough*
- *Don't deserve this much bliss, can't hold this much joy, afraid I will be bored without the drama of struggle*
- *Struggle is the path to God*
- ***Letling it all go once and for all from my spiritual, mental, and emotional energy***

Reframes

- *I am an enlightened being*
- *I am attracting and flowing divine energy*
- *I am a pillar of strength*
- *I am free of any religious shaming, I am a worthy daughter/son of God*
- *I am God's gift to the world*
- *Peace and joy are the true path to God*
- *Thank you, God, for truly loving me unconditionally*
- *God is safe, God is my friend, God is my ally*
- ***Telling the truth about who I am, breathing it in to every part of my being***
  I am worthy, I am valued, I am good enough, I am a joy in God's eyes
- *It is spiritual to receive and to give*
- *God answers my prayers, I am supported and guided in a timely way*
- *Life just keeps getting better and better, God is my ally*
- *Life is now joyful, affluent and filled with astounding blessings*
- ***This is my truth and I now claim it and live it***
- *It is spiritual to have affluence, ease, and joy, it is the way of God*
- *I am good enough and I choose to apply my best effort to what matters to me*
- *My worth has nothing to do with my results and performance in life; I am just worthy, as that is how God made me.*
- *Thank you, God, for being my friend*

- *I forgive myself, I am a remarkable human being that brings much good to the world*
- *My life is a blessing to myself and to others*

Take a deep breath while imagining filling your whole body full of light and truth. Do it two more times. Tap with both hands, using your fingertips, just below both collarbones 5-6 times. Tap on the top of your head while walking in place with a heavier stomp to ground the new energy you have activated into your body.

Clearing for Generational Patterns of Religious Abuse

This clearing script will assist you in releasing any trapped trauma energy you may carry as a result of religious abuse your ancestors may have experienced. You may not have held the beliefs or had the experiences that the script represents, yet it is a strong possibility that one of your ancestors did and you still may be the carrier of the energy pattern. If you are, it could be causing you to create unnecessary lack, pain, and struggle in your life.

Releasing all the energetic imprints of my ancestors, including...

- *Have to struggle to be religious*
- *Have to flee and hide*
- *It's dangerous having a different belief system*
- *Murdered, crucified, imprisoned for my beliefs*
- *Having to be a martyr to get what I want*
- *Persecuted for what I believe*
- *Fear of being annihilated, burning up, burning out, running, hiding*
- *Helpless, hopeless, deep grief to have to suffer so much for what I believe*

Releasing all of the old generational programming, as far back as it goes. Letting go of...

- *Scared of people in power*
- *Have to escape, afraid, people in power are hostile*
- *Attacked, have to flee, leave my home, my country*
- *Unsafe, weak boundaries, life is dangerous*

Releasing all family DNA patterns that hold religious abuse energy

- *Afraid to believe differently, I could die for believing differently*
- *Still being punished for something my ancestors experienced*
- *Releasing all of the energy patterns that I am a carrier for that cause unnecessary pain and struggle in my life due to my ancestors' religious abuse*
- *Letting it go once and for all, for myself and my posterity. It is done, it is done, it is done.*

Reframes

- *Thank you, God, I am safe now and my family is safe*
- *I am safe to believe whatever is truth for me*
- *I am living in the present*
- *I am free of all old ancestral religious abuse energy*
- *I am liberated*
- *I am creating a bright future*
- *I am centered and present in the now*
- *I am creating a life of affluence, ease, and joy*
- ***Grounding myself in the truth of the now, I am creating my experience with spirituality***
- *My energy just naturally creates the experience of affluence, ease, and joy effortlessly*
- *Life is good*
- *I am safe and free to believe and worship what is correct for me*
- *I am safe and free to enjoy life*

- *I am whole and healed and balanced*
- *I live in a safe world with many choices available to me*
- *My family is safe and free*
- **Connecting these truths with my thoughts and feelings**
- *I choose what is correct for me, and support others in choosing what is correct for them*
- *I am accountable for my actions in my lifetime and no longer accountable for the energy of my ancestors*
- *I am unconditionally loved by God and others*
- *From this moment forward I accept only truth and light at the innermost core of my being and at the level of my spiritual blueprint*

Take a deep breath while imagining filling your whole body full of light and truth. Do it two more times. Tap with both hands, using your fingertips, just below both collarbones 5-6 times. Tap on the top of your head while walking in place with a heavier stomp to ground the new energy you have activated into your body.

Clearing for Blocking or Resisting Your Soul Purpose

Your soul may be calling to you about a greater purpose—and you may not even be aware that you are blocking or resisting it! This clearing will release those conscious and subconscious blocks so you can manifest opportunities with grace and ease that your soul desires for you to have.

Thank you, God, I am ready to release...

- *Settling for less*
- *Fear of moving forward*
- *I should just be happy with what I have*
- *Fear of others judging me, who I am to want more?*
- *I don't know what to do, not even sure what I really want*
- *Nervous about making new choices*
- *Letting go of all of the...*
- *Uncertainty, confusion, what if I make a mistake? What if I go down the wrong path?*
- *Not sure how to move forward*
- *It feels safer to stay in the experience of the familiar*
- *Let it go, let it go, let it go.*
- *Letting go of all the limiting beliefs I have acquired that are keeping me from living my dreams and achieving my greatness*
- *Releasing all the lies and illusions that are keeping me stuck*
- *Scared about standing out, being noticed*
- *Frightened that I will be criticized and judged*
- *Worried what others will think of me, it's just safer to fit in and experience the status quo.*

- *Letting go of...*
- *Mediocrity, settling for less, living beneath my potential, not willing to see my greatness and my purpose*
- *Letting go of all generational beliefs passed on to me that interfere with my personal truth.*
- *Letting go of all the lies and illusions I have accepted as my personal truth*
- *Letting go of all the limitations I have imposed on myself*
- *Releasing...*
- *Afraid of doing something wrong and going too far, losing myself*
- *Let it go from every cell, let it go from my DNA.*
- *Let it go, let it go, let it go.*
- **Take a deep breath and let your body release it. Take three more deep breaths and really feel your body release it.**

Put your hand on your heart energy, the center of your chest. Repeat the following:

- *I forgive myself for having these fears and uncertainties*
- *I forgive myself for giving my power away to these illusions*
- *I forgive my mom and dad for anything they may have done to contribute to these beliefs I am ready to be free of.*
- *I forgive myself for these misunderstandings and confusion about who I am and what I am capable of.*

Reframes

- *Thank you, God...*
- *I love myself*
- *I give myself permission to make the choices that are correct for me*
- *I give my inner child permission to live her/his truth*
- *I make correct choices, it is now easy*
- *The choices I make align me with my greater purpose*
- *I am allowing my energy to create more joy, more money, more health, more of whatever I desire*
- *I am at peace with myself*
- *My purpose is first and foremost to live my truth*
- *I am open to spiritual expansion and growth*
- *My inner child is heard and understood*
- *I am on purpose in my life*
- *I am respected and honored by others as I do what is correct for me*
- *I am free of all anger energy, I have reclaimed my true self*
- *I am guided by the light, my higher self and God*
- *As I live my truth, I help everyone on this planet live theirs*
- *It is a new day of light and truth*
- *Breathing this truth into every cell of my body, thank you God...*
- *I remember my creativity and divinity*
- *I am flowing with divine energy*
- *I am balanced in every cell and my body aligns itself in divine perfection*
- *I am now calling forth and living my spiritual truth*

Take a deep breath and relax into yourself, feeling the love of God, the Universe, and your higher self. Know that God loves you and wants you to feel empowered, abundant, and successful. Turn your attention to the image in your mind of you standing in the light with God. There is a beautiful, glowing light surrounding you and nurturing you. Breath the light into every cell and fiber of your being.

As you go about your business during the day, notice that everything around you looks and feels more clear and vibrant. You are happier, other people are happier, colors are more clear and bright, you feel better and clearer, connected to your core energy, true self, and life purpose. You move through your day with a heightened sense of gratitude and appreciation, knowing you have the confidence to make decisions that are correct for you that continue to align you with your truth and purpose.

Creating Joy Meditation

Close your eyes and take a couple of deep breaths.

1. Feel the energy that is in you and around you.

2. Don't describe it. Just feel it.

3. Allow that energy to expand until it fills the whole Universe. You are that energy field and nothing is outside of you—seen and unseen.

4. Picture your Self as an outline of a figure in that energy field.

5. See and feel the energy flowing freely through the outline of you.

6. Feel the energy as the love of the Divine flowing through you.

7. As it flows through you, feel it lighten as it moves out.

8. Float on this light energy as it moves out. Feel your Self floating higher and higher. Feel the lightness as joyfulness.

9. Let the joyfulness take you to a mountain top.

10. In that joyfulness look out and see the beauty and mag-nificence, the richness and aliveness of the view wher-ever you look. You are the creator of that view.

11. Send that joyfulness into the Universe and receive it back expanded, along with more unconditional love from God that keeps flowing through the outline of you.

12. Continue to do this exercise of sending joy into the Universe and receiving it back expanded several more times.

There is energy (unconditional love) flowing through you all of the time. Just focus your attention on it. Let it come from the Universe and send it back into the Universe so that it can return energized and expanded.

This is all taking place in your imagination—the only place where you create. Since your creative imagination is unlimited, there is no limit to how magnificent your world can be. That mag-nificence is always present.

You are the creator of your world. You are the only creator of it. And you have a choice each moment how to view what you are creating. You are free to see as much beauty, richness and vitality, and to feel as much joyfulness as you desire. The more joyful you feel, the more connected you are to your true power.

You create with your thoughts and feelings. The more joyful you feel, the more joyful are your experiences, for you are creating them from your joyfulness.

Appreciate your creative power—your creative Self—for transforming your world into one of affluence, ease, and joy. Also appreciate your Self for the remarkable creative imagination you use to create a world of lack, pain, and struggle. You are a very powerful creator and you have a choice.

Remember: Both worlds exist and you are at choice to determine which world you want to live in. Use your creative power that is a joyful, harmonious and peaceful power, and you can only create joyful, harmonious and peaceful events even though beliefs you hold tell you otherwise.

Set your intention to stay in joy. Set your intention to feel deep appreciation for the creative power you are, no matter what you create.

MENTAL CLEARING SCRIPTS

Clearing for Thought Patterns of Lack, Pain, and Struggle

The thinking mind is programmed to process thoughts of lack, pain, and struggle. It wants to help you survive in the world and it needs to be trained to become an affirmative mind. This clearing will assist you in releasing some of the most age-old thoughts and beliefs that keep you in patterns of struggle. It will also help you let go of prevention thinking and support you to start the process of creation thinking.

I am ready and willing to let go of all negative thought patterns that create struggle, lack and pain, including:

- *Life is hard*
- *I have to struggle to get ahead*
- *There is never enough time*
- *We just have to learn to get by*
- *Don't expect the best*
- *Once in a lifetime opportunity*
- *I have to get used to going without*
- *It can't get any better than this*

Letting all of these limiting thoughts go for myself and my posterity, releasing...

- *I would rather die than keep dealing with this*
- *I can't stand it anymore*

- *Why does this keep happening to me?*
- *It's too good to be true*
- *Things never work out for me*
- *Don't expect it to last*
- *If something is worth it, it's worth sacrificing for*
- *No pain, no gain*

Releasing it as far back as it goes in my generations, letting go of anything I heard as a child, releasing...

- *The good probably won't happen again, it's too good to be true*
- *I am always down on my luck*
- *Prepare for the worst*

Release repeating limiting family patterns because of my negative thinking, letting go of...

- *Anger for being stuck in this pattern, frustrated and tired of it*
- *I am ready to change and afraid it won't change*
- *When are things are going to turn for me?*
- *When is my boat of good fortune coming in?*
- *What else do I have to do to make it better?*
- *Why am I still stuck?*
- *Life sucks!*
- ***Releasing these habits of thought that have been in my family for generations, it is time to let them go once and for all. I am free to now create my own story.***

Put your hand on your heart energy, the center of your chest. Repeat the following:

- *I forgive myself for thinking such negative thoughts, I am creating new habits of thought*
- *I forgive all the people who taught me to think like this*
- *I forgive humankind for continuing the story of lack, pain, and struggle, I know my choice to create joy is making a difference*

Reframes

- *Thank you, God, that I can take control of my thinking mind and train it to be a useful tool for me*
- *My mind and I are one*
- *A positive mental attitude is my natural thinking state*
- *Life supports me every day*
- *I get ahead effortlessly*
- *Time supports me, there is always enough time for what is important*
- *We get to learn how to thrive*
- *I am expecting the best*
- **Breathing in this truth, receiving it in all parts of my mind and body:**
- *There are opportunities after opportunities consistently showing up for me*
- *I have to get used to an affluent life*
- *It can get better than this and it does*
- *I am dealing with this with hope and optimism and things are getting better*

- *Wonderful things keep happening to me*
- *I am thrilled with my amazing life*
- *It's good and it is true*
- *Things always work out for me*
- *I am embracing these truths, it is my new way of thinking*
- *I expect it to keep getting better and better*
- *It's worth it and it comes to me readily*
- *I am experiencing lots of gain and lots of joy*
- *I am grateful for how much good continues to show up for me*
- *I am always up on my luck, I am such a lucky person*
- *I am preparing myself for the best*
- *I am free of patterns of lack and struggle, they are gone for good, I am now learning new life skills that help me create an affluent life*
- **Taking it all in, expanding the energetic container of me to receive more:**
- *It is changing, I am patient with the process*
- *Things are starting to turn out better for me, I am seeing it and I am grateful*
- *My boat of good fortune is landing*
- *As I believe my life will get better, it has to, that is the law of creation*
- *I am moving forward with grace and ease*
- *I attract positive because I think positive*
- *I always think of what I want*
- *Life is a remarkable adventure that is filled with affluence on all levels—lucky me!*

Open your arms to the sky, tilt your head so you are look-ing upward, and ask the heavens to open and pour down upon you the reserve of affluence energy and blessings that you have been withholding from yourself due to these old blocks. Imagine a beautiful light pouring down upon you and that you are open to receiving this higher vibration of energy. Take a deep breath while imagining filling your whole body full of light and truth. Do it two more times. Tap with both hands, using your fingertips, just below both collarbones 5-6 times. Tap on the top of your head while walking in place with a heavier stomp to ground the new energy you have activated into your body.

Clearing for Patterns of Self Sabotage

Patterns of sabotage start in the thinking mind. As you clear the limiting beliefs that keep you stuck in sabotaging yourself, you free yourself up to create successful outcomes. Clearing the energy is the first step. Following through with new life skills to create new habits will ground the energy and help you eliminate the pattern of sabotage from your life once and for all.

Before starting this clearing, bring to mind something in your life that you continue to experience the pattern of sabotaging yourself playing out. See yourself in this pattern. How does it feel? What do you say to yourself? What do you tell yourself you are going to do differently next time? Feel it, see it, and make it come to life.

Thank you, God, I am releasing my patterns of sabotaging myself, letting go of...

- *Never good enough, I always screw things up*
- *I never get what I want and it's never my fault*
- *Life is just passing me by*
- *Frustrated, tired, angry*
- *You can do better, what's wrong with you*
- *Nothing ever works out for me*
- *Procrastinating to avoid the disappointment*
- *Attracting people who take advantage of me*

Letting go of these negative patterns of thinking that create negative outcomes:

- *It doesn't matter what I do, things never work out for me*
- *Negative, sad, no point in trying*
- *Have to try harder, be more responsible*
- *If something is going to go wrong it will probably happen to me*
- *It never works out well for me*
- *Disappointing others, disappointing myself*
- *I let others down, failure, it's so embarrassing*
- ***Releasing these thoughts and beliefs once and for all:***
- *I hate disappointment*
- *Can't get hopeful*
- *Have to be prepared for something not working out, then I am not as disappointed*
- *Expect the worst and maybe something good will come of it*
- *Why try, burned out*
- *Blame, avoiding taking responsibility, that was done to me*
- *Can't seem to move forward, stuck and frustrated*
- *Stuck thinking about it, but not moving into action*

Think of all the times you have created self-sabotage and how it made you feel. Let go of the thoughts and beliefs that are keeping you stuck in recreating it. Let it go once and for all.

Put your hand on your heart energy, the center of your chest. Repeat the following:

- *I forgive myself for holding myself back and sabotaging myself*
- *I forgive myself for all of the excuses and stories I have told myself that have made it okay*
- *I am ready to change*

Reframes

- *Thank you, God, I am free to create success*
- *I am powerful, decisive, and moving forward in the right direction, taking the course of action that creates success*
- *I give up all temptation to procrastinate*
- *I think things through*
- *I do my best, I do it with confidence*
- *I imagine perfect performance for me in what I have committed to*
- *I am careful to only set up win-win situations*
- *I create success for myself*
- **Seeing it happen, believing it can happen, allowing it to happen:**
- *I am used to succeeding, it is my new norm*
- *I create every situation to be a win-win for me*
- *I am trusting the right people*
- *I am deserving the best*
- *I am free to do what I want to when I want to do it*
- *I have the power to change my life for the better*
- *I am grateful for my good fortune*

- *I am living my life fully*
- **Owning this truth for myself and my posterity:**
- *I celebrate my many successes*
- *I am open and receptive to all the support that is showing up to help me create successful outcomes*
- *It's amazing how many things show up and line up to support me in creating that which is timely and correct for me to create*
- *Breathing it into every cell of my body*

Close your eyes and take three deep breaths. Imagine yourself succeeding at a commitment you are currently pursuing. What is the outcome? What are people saying to you? What are you saying to yourself? Take a few moments and bask in the feeling of success. Come back in to present time, open your eyes, take 10-20 steps forward while repeating, "I am walking forward in to successful outcomes. I am confident and ready."

Clearing for Low Self-Esteem

This clearing will help you create a healthy self-esteem and opinion of yourself by supporting you in changing your self-talk. In order to create an affluent life, you need to have a high opinion of yourself and speak to yourself in words of affirmation and love.

Take a moment and think of the most common negative things you say to yourself and about yourself. How is having a negative opinion about yourself keeping you from creating a life you love? Find a picture of yourself as a younger child and do this clearing on behalf of this younger part of you. You started to develop a negative opinion of yourself in your childhood. Children do not have the rational understanding to see the bigger picture of their lives and identify where the true fault lies in the dysfunction they are experiencing (which is the adults in their life). So they will blame themselves and conclude that the dysfunction is their own and they are not worthy of anything better. Add your own negative self-talk phrases and thoughts to this clearing to help you let go of them.

Thank you, God, I am ready to clear my negative self-talk and negative opinion of myself, I am ready to release...

- *All of the times I put myself down*
- *All of the times I was put down as a child*
- *All of the times I apologize for myself for no good reason*
- *All of the times I felt apologetic as a child*
- *I should have done it different*
- *I should have said it different*
- *I shouldn't have done what I did*

- *Letting go of all of the distrust in myself and negative judgment*
- *Letting go of all of the distrust and negative judgment I took on from my parents*
- *Letting go of all of the times I justify, defend and explain myself*
- *Releasing all of the times I was made to feel small and insignificant as a child*

Letting go of the times I have felt...
- *Scared to be myself*
- *Hurt, rejected, and abandoned*
- *Fear of not being welcomed*
- *Not worthy of loving myself*
- *Not worthy of my parents' love and affection*
- *I need your approval to feel better about myself*
- *I needed my parents' approval to feel better about myself*
- *I am a problem, others don't like me*

Letting go of all the lies and illusions I have been telling myself for years, releasing...
- *I don't matter, I am not important*
- *Hiding my true self even from myself*
- *I am in the way, I am a bother*
- *Freeing my inner child from this negative self-perception*
- ***Releasing from my thoughts all of the negative thought patterns that perpetuate a low self-esteem, letting it go once and for all:***

Reframes

- *Think of the little child you once were and send these messages of truth to that part of you.*
- *Thank you, God, I am free, I am free, I am free*
- *I am healed, I am whole, I belong, I am wanted*
- *I am validating myself, God validates me, that is all I need to know to embrace the truth of who I am*
- *I now see myself clearly and love who I see*
- *I speak kindly to myself, I honor myself with positive self-talk*
- *Only words of self-love and self-approval flow through my thought stream*
- *When I make an error in my judgment, I notice what wants to be corrected in my actions and no longer relate it to my self-worth and opinion of myself*
- *My high opinion of myself is a constant in how I think about myself*
- *I am humble, I am grateful to be me and the opportunity God has given me to make a difference in this world*
- *Thank you God, for helping me see and think the truth of who I am*
- *I am now creating a loving, kind relationship with myself in my thoughts, I am my own best friend*
- *Thank you, God, for showing me the truth of who I am, my thoughts reflect that truth*
- *I am worthy of love and consideration*
- *As I am loving and kind to myself in my thoughts, others show me the same love and kindness*

- *I am wanted, I belong, I am open to new freedom and joy*
- *I am looking forward to the future, life is good*

Take a deep breath while imagining filling your whole body full of light and truth. Do it two more times. Tap with both hands, using your fingertips, just below both collarbones 5-6 times. Tap on the top of your head while walking in place with a heavier stomp to ground the new energy you have activated into your body.

A supportive exercise would be to write all of the positive reframes on the picture of yourself as a younger child. This will support you in making the connection in your mind that the words represent the truth of your inner child, which will help that part of you integrate that truth.

EMOTIONAL CLEARING SCRIPTS

Clearing for Emotional Shaming in Childhood

If you were taught that feelings are unacceptable when you were a child, this clearing will help you connect with your emotional energy and support you in feeling all of your feelings.

Thank you, God, for helping me clear all of the shame I have carried around in my feelings, I am ready to let go of...

- *Feelings are bad*
- *Stop feeling that way*
- *Letting go of all the times I have apologized for crying*
- *It's not manly to feel my feelings*
- *Emotions are a weakness*

Letting go of all the shaming references about feelings that I heard as a child, including...

- *I'll give you something to cry about*
- *Crying makes you unattractive*
- *Stop whining and crying*
- *I am going to leave you here if you don't stop whining and fussing*
- *Stop being such a drama queen*
- *What are you fussing about?*
- *You'll be ugly forever and no one will ever love you if you don't stop crying*
- *You're just crying to manipulate me*

- *Out there in the real world, people don't cry when they get upset, you'll never make it out there*

Letting go of...
- *All of the unexpressed buried emotion including sadness, anger, and grief*
- *I have to suppress my feelings so I don't upset my mom*
- *I have to suppress my feelings so I don't upset my dad*
- *Don't want to be the problem child*
- *Mom's emotions are more important than my emotional needs*
- *Dad's emotional needs are more important than my emotional needs*
- *Putting my feelings aside, it's okay, it's really not bothering me*
- *Lying about how I really feel so others don't get upset at me*

Freeing myself of all the fear of feeling my feelings, letting go of...
- *You should know how I feel, can't you tell?*
- *It's your job to figure out how I am really feeling!*
- *Can't put words to how I feel, it's safer to keep it all inside*
- *If I don't feel it, maybe it will go away*
- *Stuffing all the emotional energy inside my body*
- *Getting sick and tired due to all of the pent up emotion inside of me*
- *It's not safe to feel my feelings*
- *Holding it in until I lose control*
- ***Let it go, let it go, let it go!***

Put your hand on your heart energy, the center of your chest.
Repeat the following:

- *I forgive myself for carrying this emotional shame for so long*
- *I forgive my parents, they did the best they knew how, considering they were also shamed*

Reframes

- *Thank you, God, it is now safe to feel my feelings*
- *I am in charge of my emotional self*
- *I am learning to express how I feel, others listen and understand*
- *It is my job to be the manager of my own feelings*
- *I am feeling all of my feelings and I am a good person*
- *My inner child had a right to feel her/his feelings*
- *I am a strong, wise person for feeling all there is to feel*
- *I manage my emotional self wisely and with maturity*
- *My inner child is now safe to feel all there is to feel*
- *I allow my feelings to flow*
- *When I cry, I honor my tears*
- *As I feel my sadness, anger, grief, I open myself to feel joy, happiness and love*
- *My emotions are powerful tools that support me in creating a life I love*
- *I am emotionally healthy*
- *I am growing myself up emotionally*
- *I am grateful for my inner child and all of the unfelt emotion they have carried, they are now free to feel all of their feelings*

- *I am trusting my feelings, they are a powerful tool for good in my life*
- *Thank you, God, for assisting me on this emotional healing journey*
- *I am safe to explore my feelings*
- *As I respect how I feel, others show me the same respect*
- *I respect others' feelings*
- *I choose to create boundaries with people who do not manage their feelings with respect to others*

Take a deep breath while imagining filling your whole body full of light and truth. Do it two more times. Tap with both hands, using your fingertips, just below both collarbones 5-6 times. Tap on the top of your head while walking in place with a heavier stomp to ground the new energy you have activated into your body.

Clearing for Emotional Addictions

We subconsciously can use emotion to manipulate people and situations, to try and get support and be understood. As emotions are meant to support us in feeling good, and to also be used as a navigation tool to help us make decisions, using them for other purposes can be a hindrance to what they are designed to be used for. This clearing will help you stop the pattern of misusing your emotions in ways that will only create more lack, pain, and struggle in your life.

Thank you, God, for helping me release all of my patterns of emotional addiction, including...
- *Nobody would notice me if I don't get emotional*
- *Putting up emotional walls to punish you*
- *Overreacting to get back at you*
- *You're not listening so I am going to get upset so you will listen to me*
- *I won't let you know how I feel because you don't really care*
- *You had your chance to support me emotionally, but now it's too late*
- *I'll just keep it to myself*
- *Sad my emotional needs are not met, still looking for someone to meet them*
- *It's your job to take care of me emotionally, don't you know that*

Releasing and letting go of...
- *The only way I will get my way is if I am sad or upset*
- *Now you will listen to me, now that I am getting emotional about it*
- *My needs are not met*
- *Emotion gets me attention*
- *Angry that I lose control*
- *Nobody listens to me until I get angry*
- *Using anger to get my way*
- *Using sadness to get noticed*
- *Feeling empty if I don't feel all of this pent up emotion*
- ***Ending the pattern of...***
- *Don't know how to use words to ask for what I want*
- *Pouting so you will ask me what's wrong*
- *It's your job to read my emotions and then reach out to me*
- *Angry when you don't notice I am upset*
- *Didn't get my emotional needs met as a child, looking to you to take care of me emotionally now*
- *What's wrong with you, don't you know I need your emotional support, why should I have to ask for it*
- *If you really loved me, you would know how I feel*
- *Getting upset at customer service reps so I get them to listen to me*
- *If I don't get upset as a customer when there is a problem the problem won't be taken seriously*
- ***Let it all go once and for all***

Reframes

- *Thank you, God, I am growing up emotionally*
- *I am using my feelings in healthy, supportive ways that add peace and happiness to my life*
- *I am in charge of my emotional self*
- *I am sharing how I feel when appropriate, positive outcomes result from it*
- *It is safe to feel my feelings*
- *I give myself attention and receive attention from others*
- *I am in control of my feelings, I manage them wisely*
- *I am emotionally balanced and calm and I am heard*
- *When it is correct for me, things go my way, and I stay calm*
- *I feel full of joy and peace and it is familiar*
- *I am noticed for the good person I am*
- *The appropriate words come to me to share how I am feeling*
- *When I need emotional support, I ask for it and I receive it*
- *I always create positive experiences and outcomes when dealing with customer issues that I need resolved.*
- *I am forgiving myself for all of the times I have behaved poorly in managing my emotions*

Take a deep breath while imagining filling your whole body full of light and truth. Do it two more times. Tap with both hands, using your fingertips, just below both collarbones 5-6 times. Tap on the top of your head while walking in place with a heavier stomp to ground the new energy you have activated into your body.

Clearing to Heal Your Inner Child

This clearing will assist you in releasing any shame energy that you still hold in your emotional energy field. As you use the metaphor of an inner child still carrying around the shame-based beliefs you took on as truth in your younger years, you will be able to see that child set free to live in the wholeness of truth they have always been worthy of living in. Before doing this clearing, find a picture of a younger you—whatever age comes to mind. Choose any age from your infancy, up to your teen years. Imagine giving the gift of this clearing to that part of you. You can do this clearing multiple times with a reference to a different age, as we take on different shame-based beliefs and emotions throughout our childhood. You may also benefit from the clearings available at my Online Healing Center that focus on specific age groups and the emotional and developmental needs you moved through as a child that still may need to be addressed in your healing work.

Thank you, God, I am ready to heal the child within me from all shame based beliefs and emotions, releasing the belief

- *I am not good enough*
- *I am the cause of all the trouble*
- *No matter what I do it's never good enough*
- *I am the reason Mom and Dad are not happy*
- *It's my job to make things better for the whole family*
- *Want to get away and hide, can't get away, stuck, lonely, lost*
- ***Releasing all of the times I felt embarrassed to be me, all of the times I didn't want to live anymore, letting go of:***

- *Taking on the dysfunctional energy of the family, maybe that will help everyone feel better*

Releasing my childhood self of the need to show up to be the healer in the family before I am ready and mature enough to be:

- *Subconsciously I know I have an important role to play here, the only thing I can do to make it better is take on my family's shameful energy—because I am just a little child*
- *Playing the healer role too soon, too early, releasing my child self from this role!*
- ***Letting it all go!***
- *Have to hide my true feelings to avoid adding to the upset*
- *Have to take care of Mom, have to take care of Dad, putting myself aside*
- *Releasing all of the sadness and fear that my needs don't matter*
- *Fear of speaking up, speaking my truth, just say what others want me to say*
- *Letting go of all the teasing, the taunting, the bullying, the feeling of powerlessness*
- *Letting my inner child be free of the compromise, discontent, lack of joy*
- *I never got to be a child, had to grow up too fast*
- *Have to protect the family and hide my pain*
- *Not sure who I am any more*
- *Letting go of all the energy I took on from Mom*
- *Letting go of all the energy I took on from Dad*

- *Letting go of all the energy I took on from other family members*
- *Releasing once and for all the family patterns of lack, pain, and struggle that my inner child is still stuck living in, freeing that part of me to now experience affluence, ease and joy*
- *It's time to heal and let my inner child have the joy she/he is designed for*

Reframes

- *Thank you, God, I am free to be myself*
- *It is safe to be a child*
- *There is joy in being me, just being me*
- *I am feeling my feelings, my feelings count*
- *Making the connections of truth inside my entire being*
- *I am glad to be alive*
- *I have a strong sense of belonging*
- *I am understanding that my parents' issues were theirs and not mine*
- *I am staying in my own energy*
- *My child self is free to be happy and healthy*
- *My child self is now safe and secure within me*
- *I am the new healthy parent that will support my inner child's needs being met*
- *I am understanding the issues in my family had nothing to do with me*
- *I am getting my needs met easily*
- *I am feeling and processing all of my emotions*
- *I am happy to be me*

- *I am claiming the truth of my authentic child self, making that connection on all levels of my being*
- *I am glad I am a girl/boy*
- *I am loved unconditionally*
- *I am accepted and supported in moving forward in my own journey*
- *Thank you, God*
- *I am trusting myself*
- *I am free to play and have fun*
- *I am taking all of the time I need to grow and take on my adult roles*
- *I am standing in my own truth and energy*
- *I am safe to explore this world*
- *I am starting new things that interest me, my interests count*
- *I am cherished and nurtured*
- *Thank you, God, I am perfect as you created me*

Take a deep breath while imagining filling your whole body full of light and truth. Do it two more times. Tap with both hands, using your fingertips, just below both collarbones 5-6 times. Tap on the top of your head while walking in place with a heavier stomp to ground the new energy you have activated into your body. Imagine embracing your child self in your arms and bringing that energy into your heart to be safe and secure within you.

Visualization to Grow Yourself Up Emotionally

This visualization will help you integrate all of the energies of your emotional self between birth and your teen years. These were the years you were most vulnerable to either learning to accept and express your emotional self, or to deny and repress your emotional self. Doing this visualization will help you reset your emotional energy to allow you to feel safe and confident in feeling and expressing what emotion is true for you.

Sit in a comfortable position with your arms and legs uncrossed. Take three deep breaths and with each exhale, let go of any thoughts running through your mind. Notice your whole body from the top of your head to the bottoms of your feet.

Close your eyes and turn your energy inward. Imagine you are standing in the light of heaven with guides and/or angels there to support you. Imagine yourself turning in the direction of your past. See a timeline extending all the way into your past, all the way back to your birth. Your guides/angels take you by the hand and you easily and quickly glide all the way back along your time-line to the beginning of your life to the place of your birth. You find your infant self there, waiting for you. You pick up this little baby and tell her/him how glad you are to see them and that you are emotionally bringing them home to you today. Cuddle that little one and tell your little self how much you love yourself. Tell them, "You are loved and wanted because you were born. There is nothing you have to DO to be loved." Embrace this infant self and meld the image and energy of your infant self into your heart.

Move along the timeline until you see another younger part of yourself between the ages of two or three years old. This little toddler that is you has been waiting for you. Bend down on your knees so you can look this little self in the eyes and invite them to come to you as you open your arms to them. Tell this little toddler self, "It is safe for you to explore this world and see how you feel about it. Your feelings are always safe with me." Embrace this little one and imagine the image and energy of this little self melding into you heart.

Move further along the timeline until you find the part of you that is between four and six years old. This is the part of you that started to go to school and learn about the world around you. Say hello to this younger self and let them know how glad you are to see them. They have been waiting for you and are eager to have your support. Bend down to talk to this younger self and tell them, "It is safe to think for yourself and have your own ideas and opinions and I will always love you and support you." This little one has a big smile on their face and is so grateful to feel emotionally supported by you to live true to who they are. Embrace this little one and imagine the image and energy of this part of you melding in to your heart.

As you continue along your timeline, you find an older part of you, your grade school self. You notice a you are growing and by this time in your life have decided if the world is safe place to share your true feelings. This part of you is between seven and twelve years old. This part of you may be hesitant to come to you depending on how much they trust adults. Let this part of you know who you are. "Hello, I am your adult self, I have come to take you home to be safe within my heart where you are free to feel whatever you need to feel." This part of you feels reassured as you walk toward each other. Bend over and give this part of you a hug and tell them, "You have a right to be your own person, you can try out different roles and ways of using your personal power." This part of you feels a weight come off their shoulders as they are now free to live for themselves, rather than adapting to live for everyone else—especially Mom and Dad. As you embrace this part of you, imagine the image and energy of this self melding into your heart.

You look back to your birth and see how far you've come as you now move along your timeline to the time of your teenage years. You find your teenage self that is between the age of 13-20, the maturing part of you that is becoming an adult. You say hello and introduce yourself. This part of you is curious why you are there. You let them know that you weren't given the proper emotional support to enter into adulthood, feeling emotionally confident and mature. You are here to help make up the difference. You take this part of you by the hand and give them a hug while you affirm to them, "You can know who you are and learn through your choices how you feel about people and experiences. You can take all the time you need to grow up and prepare yourself for your adult life." This part of you feels reassured and supported by you. Bring this part of you close to you, and imagine the image and energy of this teenage self melding into your heart.

You see where you are on your timeline in relationship to the now of your life. You can glide along the timeline in the direction of the now. As you move along, you are like a magnet, attracting all the emotional parts of you that you split from throughout your adult years. This energy melds into your being, coming into balance and harmony with the truth of who you are. You arrive back at the point of now and take a deep breath. Open your eyes and stand up, marching in place or going for a walk to help your body integrate this emotional energy into your entire body and being.

PHYSICAL CLEARING SCRIPTS

Clearing to End the Battle with Pain

Experiencing the pattern of battling pain is a common dynamic. Many factors have influenced this mindset, including family, society, and medical culture. It is a common experience to perceive the constant issue of pain in the body as something we have to fight and try to win. The problem is, we only create the pain having more life force and presence when we "fight" it, as we invoke it to have more power to fight us back. Letting go of the battle, the fight, and war with pain will allow peaceful solutions and the energy of love to be expressed, which will allow pain to return to its original energy—love.

I am ready to release the following beliefs, I am letting go of...
- *Pain is my enemy*
- *Fighting pain for a long time*
- *My body has failed me and let me down*
- *Even though I feel like I battle with my pain, I am choosing to end this battle*
- *Releasing pain is my enemy*
- *I am always battling pain*
- *The battle never ends*
- *I can't have peace until the battle is over*
- *Trying to win the battle against pain and feel like I am always losing*

- *Can't stand it, giving into the pain, it's more powerful than me*
- *I am never going to win, it's a losing battle*
- **Let it go, let it go, let it go**
- *Letting go of all the limiting beliefs I have acquired in my life about pain being a battle*
- *Letting go of all the lies and stories that have created the illusion that I am at war with pain and my body*
- *Letting go of all the times I have said or thought, "I have to fight this pain"*
- *Letting go of all the times I have felt defeated, it's a losing battle, a battle I can never win*
- *Letting go of the battle energy, the energetic pattern of pain is my enemy*
- *Let it go from every cell of my body, every joint, every muscle, every organ, every part of my body that has carried the belief for me that pain is a battle, a war, an enemy*
- **Let it go, let it go, let it go**
- *Take a deep breath and let your body release it. Take three more deep breaths and really feel your body release it.*

Put your hand on your heart energy, the center of your chest. Repeat the following:
- *I forgive myself for being at war with my pain, I have always done the best I know how*
- *I forgive myself for believing pain is my enemy, I didn't really know any better. But now I do!*

- *I forgive any doctors and health professionals for supporting this mindset*
- *I forgive the pain for disrupting my life*

Reframes
- *I love myself*
- *I am at peace with my pain*
- *I can choose to love my pain now, because I know love is more powerful and will help my pain heal*
- *I am becoming an ally to my pain*
- *I am now choosing to create a body that loves and supports me*
- *I am listening and learning from my pain*
- *It is a great teacher, a great ally to me*
- *I am open to my life changing*
- *I am willing to look at other issues in my life once the pain is gone*
- *I am experiencing my pain retreating*
- *I am choosing peace every day, regardless of how much pain is there*
- *I welcome my pain and invite it in, I am working in partnership with my pain to find peaceful solutions to resolving it*
- *I am grateful the battle is over*
- *I am grateful for my healing*
- *I choose peace and happiness now*

If you could visualize your pain, what would it look like? Is it a person, male or female? Is it an animal, a shape, or a symbol? Imagine your pain comes to life. Give it a shape and a form. (Whatever shows up will give you more insight into what your pain represents from your childhood and may give you more insights on what you need to clear.)

Now that you have given your pain an identity, say hello to it and thank it. Give your pain a high five. See you and your pain both throw in the towel, or wave a white flag of surrender. See yourself surrendering to your pain and your pain surrendering to you and then coming together to work things out.

Every time your pain is trying to get your attention, from this moment forward, greet it with open arms, say, "There you are! I love you and accept you. You are showing me that there is a part of me that is still in pain about being me. I now choose to love you. Let's sit and talk. What is it you want me to know?"

As you do this, you will find your pain releasing and letting go, because anything or any part of us that knows that it is loved returns to the love that it is.

Clearing to Release Disease and Illness

This clearing will help you release any hidden attachments you may have of needing your illness, or any limiting beliefs that you hold consciously and subconsciously that keep your body from healing.

I am freeing my body of any blocks and resistance that is keeping it from healing, I am releasing...
- *Chronic illness*
- *My illness has become my identity*
- *Afraid I can't heal*
- *Looking for the answers to healing outside of me*
- *What's wrong with my body*
- *Angry at my body*
- *It just keeps falling apart*

Letting go of all the following and anything else known or unknown to me, releasing...
- *I need my illness to get my emotional needs met*
- *Who am I without my sickness?*
- *I like the extra attention it gets me*
- *At least the doctors listen to me*
- *The nurses are like my surrogate parent*
- *Depressed*
- *Depressed body*
- *I don't really want to get better, who would I be without this disease?*

Letting it all go once and for all, releasing...
- *Tired of being sick*
- *Sick and tired*
- *Talking about it all the time*
- *Referencing it when anyone asks me how I am*
- *It's become a big part of my life story*
- *I don't know how to listen to my body*
- *My body forgot how to heal*
- *My body is my enemy*
- *Letting go of the pattern of my body being sick and tired all of the time*
- *Let it go once and for all*

Put your hand on your heart energy, the center of your chest. Repeat the following:
- *I forgive myself for any emotional needs I may have attached to my illness, I now know I can have my needs met in healthy ways*
- *I forgive my body, it's doing the best it knows how*
- *I forgive my illness, it has been a great teacher and now I can let it go*

Reframes

- *Thank you, God.*
- *Self-healing is natural*
- *My body responds to the resources I am guided to support it with*
- *My body heals, I am healthy, I am strong*
- *I forgive myself for being sick*
- *I am listening to my body, it directs me to the correct resources to receive the healing support it needs*
- *I love my body*
- *My body is now healthy and well*
- *I have a strong and able body*
- *I enjoy my body*
- *I move easily in my healthy, strong body*
- *My body is my friend*
- *Health and vitality are my natural state*
- *I am allowing my body to create this new story of health*
- *I am having fun in my body*
- *My body speaks to me and I listen*
- *Thank you, God, I am grateful for the gift of my strong, healthy body*

Take a deep breath while imagining filling your whole body full of light and truth. Do it two more times. Tap with both hands, using your fingertips, just below both collarbones 5-6 times. Tap on the top of your head while walking in place with a heavier stomp to ground the new energy you have activated into your body.

FINANCIAL CLEARING SCRIPTS

Clearing for Financial Lack

This clearing will help you clear your money issues. It helps remove blocks relating to allowing more flow and accumulation of money into your life.

I now release to the light any and all programming that keeps me stuck in creating a lack of money, I am letting go of...
- *Never enough money*
- *Feel like a victim to money*
- *Money doesn't grow on trees*
- *Money is filthy and dirty*
- *Money is evil*
- *Rich people are crooks*
- *If I have a lot of money, I'll be worldly and stuck up*

Letting go of all the generational patterns I have been carrying with money, including...
- *I will never make enough money*
- *Always more money going out than coming in*
- *Feeling frustrated, angry, tired of this struggle with money*

Releasing...
- *Don't deserve wealth*
- *Have to work hard to get ahead*
- *Money is difficult to come by*

- *Only greedy people have money*
- *I couldn't ever charge that much*
- *They're only doing it for the money*
- *Not good enough to make money*
- *Money is hard*
- *Money only comes from hard work*

Releasing from every cell of my body all the old money programming, letting go of...
- *Negative money thinking*
- *Always speaking in terms of lack of money*
- *I can't afford it*
- *Have to save for a rainy day*
- *A penny saved is a penny earned*
- *A depression could come any day*

Releasing all of the lies and illusions I heard my parents share about money, letting go of...
- *Never talk about money*
- *Never tell people how much money you have*
- *Keep money a secret*
- *Poor people can never get out from under*
- *My parents could never get ahead, neither will I*
- *I get ahead financially but something always shows up to set me back*
- *I am letting this old money story go once and for all*

Put your hand on your heart energy, the center of your chest.
Repeat the following:

- *I forgive myself for creating my financial lack, I have been doing the best I know how and I am ready to do better*
- *I forgive myself for blaming money*
- *I forgive money, it wants to show up for me now*
- *I forgive my parents and ancestors for handing down these old money stories, it's time to let them go*

Reframes

- ***Thank you, God, I am...***
- *Ready to create my own story of abundance with money*
- *I am experiencing an increase in my flow and accumulation of money*
- *I am a good manager of money*
- *Money loves me and I love money*
- *Money is my friend and support*
- *I continue to increase my financial affluence*
- *Money just grows and grows for me*
- *Money is easy to come by*
- ***Thank you, God...***
- *I am abundant in money*
- *I deserve financial affluence*
- *There is always enough money and more*
- *I am grounded with money*
- *I am allowing more money to flow to me*
- *I am managing my increase wisely*
- *I get the help I need if it supports me*

- *I am creating my own story of financial affluence, I am grateful*

Take a deep breath while imagining filling your whole body full of light and truth. Do it two more times. Tap with both hands, using your fingertips, just below both collarbones 5-6 times. Tap on the top of your head while walking in place with a heavier stomp to ground the new energy you have activated into your body.

General Clearing for Creating a Life of Lack, Pain, and Struggle

Every day, people keep themselves in lack and pain, due to small habits and choices. Little do they know that these daily habits keep them blocked from connecting to their potential to create a life of affluence, ease, and joy. This clearing will help you clear some of your basic limiting beliefs that keep you from creating a rich and affluent life, which includes financial affluence.

Releasing the old programs, including...

- *I have to give up myself in order to fit in*
- *It's selfish to consider myself and choose myself*
- *I have to live in struggle and pain to fit in*
- *Still running my family's story and energy*
- *Releasing this old energy*
- *It's worldly to experience pleasure*
- *Settling for mediocrity*
- *Speaking in terms of lack and struggle*
- *Caught in the collective energy of lack and struggle*
- *Looking outside myself for answers*
- *Release this old programming*
- *Who am I to make make a difference?*
- *I have to help others before I help myself*
- *Others' needs and pleasures are more important than mine*

Letting go of...

- *I have to say yes when I mean no*
- *Giving my power away to these old roles*
- *Still playing off old family scripts*
- *Not knowing what is correct, letting what I think others want dictate what is correct for me*
- *Can't trust my own intuition*
- *Still trying to get my emotional needs met by giving up my own power*
- *Releasing these old programs of who I am supposed to be*

Put your hand on your heart energy, the center of your chest. Repeat the following:

- *I forgive myself for doubting myself.*
- *I forgive myself for accepting lack and struggle as my way of life*
- *I forgive myself for settling for mediocrity*
- *I forgive myself for looking outside myself and drowning my soul's promptings by giving my power to others.*

Reframes

- *Thank you, God...*
- *It is safe to live my life in affluence, ease, and joy*
- *I speak about my life in terms of affluence, ease, and joy*
- *I am abundant*
- *My life flows with ease*
- *I am creating and experiencing joy more and more each day*
- *As I choose myself, I have more to give*
- *I make choices that are correct for me first*
- *I am creating my own story*
- *I am creating my own story with money*
- *I deserve wealth*
- *I use my riches wisely*
- *I am on purpose with my life*
- *My soul is guiding me*
- *I turn within to seek my answers*
- *I am still*
- *In the stillness, the answers are loud and clear*
- *It is safe to move forward with what is correct for me*
- *I am feeling the love and comfort of my soul's energy*
- *I am on purpose*
- *One of my greatest purposes is to live a life of affluence, ease and joy.*
- *God wants me to thrive and share my gifts with others*
- *I receive and then have more to give*
- *My true purpose is already validated by God*
- *I am allowing pleasure and celebrating the pleasure of others*
- *I am comfortable with this new order of energy*

- *All is well*
- *Life is good*
- *I am blessed*
- *I live my purpose of affluence, ease, and joy*

Take a deep breath while imagining filling your whole body full of light and truth. Do it two more times. Tap with both hands, using your fingertips, just below both collarbones 5-6 times. Tap on the top of your head while walking in place with a heavier stomp to ground the new energy you have activated into your body.

RELATIONSHIP CLEARING SCRIPTS

Clearing for Relationship Issues

This clearing will help you clear both the conscious and subconscious beliefs you may carry about what is expected of you or what you expect of your partner in your relationship.

Letting go of all the relationship beliefs and patterns that are keeping us stuck, releasing...

- *I don't exist*
- *Have to keep up appearances*
- *I need to control things to feel safe in my relationship*
- *Afraid to express my real self in fear I will be shot down*
- *Don't know how to love or to be vulnerable*
- *Afraid to love and be intimate*
- *Fear of being rejected and hurt*
- *Can't stand up for myself*

Releasing the lies and illusions I may have about relationships, letting go of...

- *How can I let you love me when I don't even love myself?*
- *Feeling powerless in my relationship*
- *My partner's needs are more important than mine*
- *Distrust*
- *Have to focus on the needs of my partner first*
- *Shame myself*
- *Avoid asking for support*
- *Settling for less, because they don't want anything better*

- *No hope, no boundaries, always the victim*
- *Have to work at being loved*
- *If I let you down, I will lose you*
- *Fear of abandonment*
- *Fear of rejection*
- *Afraid to ask for what I need*

Letting go of...

- *Unreasonable expectations of myself and my partner*
- *Repeating my parents' pattern in my own relationship*
- *I have to feel bad for you*
- *I alter my truth in the hope it will create more harmony in my relationship*

Releasing any beliefs and perceptions that keep me and my partner from changing, including...

- *They'll never change*
- *It's just the way they are*
- *I know what they are going to say and do*
- *They're not interested in working things out*
- *They think this is all airy-fairy*

Letting go of all the patterns of...

- *Poor communication*
- *Nobody really listens to the other*
- *Needing to be heard, never feel heard and understood*
- *Not taking the time to learn better communication skills*
- *It requires too much work*

Letting go of...
- *Problems with intimacy*
- *Sex with contempt*
- *Letting it all go once and for all*
- *Blaming myself and others*

Put your hand on your heart energy, the center of your chest. Repeat the following:
- *I forgive myself for blaming my partner*
- *I know they're doing the best they know how*
- *I forgive my partner for blaming me*
- *I'm doing the best I know how*

Reframes
- ***Thank you, God...***
- *I can now enjoy relationships*
- *My needs and desires are important*
- *It is safe to be intimate with my partner*
- *I am a great communicator*
- *We are committed to learning better communication skills*
- *My relationship is growing as a result of the healthy communication skills my partner and I use on a regular basis*
- *It is safe to be myself in my relationship*
- *I speak what is true for me and I am heard and understood*

Taking a deep breath and breathing in these truths...

- *I am open and it is safe to be loved*
- *My partner and I share a pleasurable and enjoyable sexual relationship*
- *I exist, I am important, I am the real me in my relationship*
- *We honor each other*
- *I am creating a healthy partnership with my spouse*
- *Both our needs matter*
- *My relationship just keeps getting better and better*
- *Letting myself believe and trust this, it is my new relationship story*

Take a deep breath while imagining filling your whole body full of light and truth. Do it two more times. Tap with both hands, using your fingertips, just below both collarbones 5-6 times. Tap on the top of your head while walking in place with a heavier stomp to ground the new energy you have activated into your body.

Clearing for Taking On Other People's Energy

There is a lot of negative, heavy energy going around these days. How do you know if what you are feeling is really yours? Maybe it's the person you are living with, or a close friend. Maybe you picked up someone else's energy at a gathering you recently attended or at work. Maybe you were affected by a TV show or a movie. And, maybe you're running energy you took on from a parent in your childhood that has been with you your entire life! This clearing will help you clear away the emotions and beliefs that you took on in your childhood that set you up to be vulnerable to the negative energies of other people and places. You will also learn how to strengthen your own personal energy system so it is not susceptible to taking on other people's energy. I have had to personally learn to do it for myself over the years without compromising my empathic gifts and intuitive talents.

Let's start with a visualization. Close your eyes, take three deep breaths, and begin to relax your body. Notice your entire body as you breathe in light and peace, saying relax, relax, relax. Repeat in your mind or out loud, the following intention:

I am letting go of any negative energy that is not mine. I release it to return to its proper owner and creator. I send this back to them with love and awareness. I am now free to experience my own energy, my own self, my own being.

I am now choosing to release and let go of...

- *Any energy I have been taking on that is not mine*
- *Not even knowing what energy is mine and what is not mine*
- *Paying a price for taking on the energy of others*
- *Angry that I took on other people's energy, it's time to let it go.*

Releasing...

- *It's not mine, it is mine, how do I know the difference?*
- *Energetic confusion*
- *Taking on negative energy is my habit*
- *Running other people's negative emotions*
- *Taking on the negative thoughts of others*
- *Making my body sick*

Releasing playing this role...

- *I was just trying to help my parents feel better*
- *I just wanted a happier home*
- *Nobody else was taking responsibility for the energy*
- ***Letting go of...***
- *Taking on my partner's energy*
- *Always trying to make it better for both of us*
- *They're not willing to be accountable for it, so I guess I have to be*
- *Let it go once and for all*
- *It is time, I am ready*
- *I am ready to let go of this role, once and for all*

Visualize yourself as a small child and invite that child to let go of this old role. Tell them they don't need to take on the energy of your parents, family, and other people anymore. Surround them with white light and protection. Invite them to go play and have fun and learn about who they are and their energy and gifts.

Reframes

- *Thank you, God...*
- *I am ready to know myself and feel my own energy*
- *I am getting stronger and stronger in holding my own*
- *I am free to be me and run only my energy*
- *I am stable in my own energy*
- *It feels good to be me*
- *I am letting others be responsible for their energy and what their energy creates*
- *It feels good*
- *I am responsible for my energy and what my energy creates*
- *I am taking care of my energy by avoiding all music, television or movies that energetically compromises me*
- *I am avoiding people who compromise me*
- *I am taking care of myself in my intimate relationships by using these techniques*
- *Thank you, God...*
- *I am confident*
- *I feel great*
- *I am me and they are them*
- *I am knowing the difference*

Imagine a situation where you have felt vulnerable, where you sense you take on someone else's energy. Imagine yourself with that person. You are surrounded by large reflecting panels all around you. You are standing in the center of these reflection panels and all the energy of the other person is just being reflected back to them and you are safe and secure in your own energetic space.

- *Take three deep breaths and notice your own body, your own feelings, your own thoughts, your own energetic space. Feel the peace of you.*
- *Zip up your energy by pretending you have a zipper that runs up from your pubic bone to your bottom lip and zip it up three times.*
- *Enjoy being you. You and your unique energy are a gift to the world.*

6-Step Process for Clearing Relationship Upsets

Think of something in the last few days that your partner did that triggered you emotionally.

List the upset here:

Describe how you responded:

Most people's first response is to put their focus outward to their partner and events that played out in the scenario that upset them. You feel all this emotional energy rise up and you take that energy and project it outward to the story that is playing out in your life and the other person in the story. You want to "do" something about it: blame your partner, fix it, change it, or take some form of action. As you do that, you are actually flowing this potently charged emotional energy into your life story to set you up to experience it again. You are creating more of what you don't want by flowing this energy into the outer experience.

The truth is, your upset is a set up. The problem is, you are focusing your energy and attention in the wrong direction to try and permanently change these struggles from showing up again.

Experiences of lack, pain, and struggle in your relationship will keep showing up if you project all of that emotionally charged energy outwardly. The trick is to go within and follow these simple, yet often challenging steps:

1. Acknowledge you are upset to yourself.
2. Recognize you are repeating a pattern.
3. Release the messenger of your upset—your partner, who is just playing a role for you.
4. Feel your feelings as you take deep cleansing breaths.
5. Allow the energy of your feelings to come to a state of neutral.
6. Write down what you would like to experience in place of this.

List what you would like to experience in place of the upset:

These six simple steps are incredibly powerful and will shift your upsets to become moments of powerful transformational tools in your life.

Now imagine this same upset and imagine yourself going through these six simple steps.

How do you feel?

What do you want to create instead?

Trying to change your physical experience by fixing your outer world is like pulling weeds and not getting the root of the weed out. The weed is going to come back. The upset is an effect. The cause is your old energy of lack, pain, and struggle that you keep recycling. Remember, you are choosing to upgrade your humanity to the energy of affluence, ease, and joy. And it takes repeating these steps over and over to do it.

Clearing Your Relationship Energy Centers

Your chakra energy is a powerful energy system that influences your life experience. In your personal energy system, these vortices of energy are going through a shift. This energy shift is helping you become more conscious of your ability to create a life of affluence, ease, and joy. This clearing will help you consciously assist in this shift. It is not necessary to understand the chakra system to be a beneficiary of this clearing. This clearing focuses on the lower three chakra energy centers that assist us in either creating lack, pain, and struggle, or affluence, ease, and joy in our relationship and family experiences.

To start this clearing, bring attention to your lower chakra energies, which are energy stations in your personal energy body that vibrate in the lower half of your body. These energy centers hold old cultural and family system programming that is opening and clearing.

Set the intention that these energy centers will open and clear as you repeat this clearing script.

- *Close your eyes and get in touch with your body. Notice your breath. Put your attention on the lower half of your torso, the area between the pubic bone and your chest.*
- *Your first chakra is in the area of your pubic bone. This energy supports you in your family and cultural experience, which is going through a big shift right now from the experience of people giving themselves up for the survival of the tribe, to now reclaiming yourself to begin to thrive and help others thrive.*
- *Place your hand on this energy center and see it infused with the color red, helping to open and activate this energy center.*

Repeat the following:
- *Releasing the old program that I have to help others to have value*
- *I have to give up myself in order to fit in*
- *I have to lose myself in the service of others in order to be pleasing to God*
- *It's selfish to consider myself and choose myself*
- *Releasing this old energy*

Now move your hand to the middle of your abdomen. This is the area of your second chakra. This energy supports you in creating your life, and experiencing pleasure.

The old energy you are letting go of is personal sacrifice and giving up pleasure as the sacred path. The new energy is receiving and giving pleasure. Its sacred and life force energy is meant to be used to create pleasure. Imagine the color orange infusing and opening this energy center.

Repeat the following: Releasing...
- *It's worldly to experience pleasure*
- *I have to help others before I help myself*
- *Others' needs and pleasures are more important than mine*
- *Feeling selfish and superficial to think of myself first*
- *It feels wrong*
- *Uncomfortable*
- *Uneasy*
- *Let it go*

Now move your hand to the area just above your navel, the area of your third chakra. This energy expresses your personal power.

The old program was that power was used to control and create hierarchy, that only a few could succeed. The new energy you are opening is an even playing field. Everyone has the right to thrive and your power is your life force to create that with. Imagine the color yellow infusing and opening this energy center.

Repeat the following: Letting go of...

- *I have to say yes when I mean no*
- *Giving my power away to these old roles*
- *Not knowing what is correct, letting what I think others want dictate what is correct for me*
- *Can't trust my own decisions*
- *Looking outside myself for answers*
- *Still trying to get my emotional needs met by giving up my own power*
- *Releasing these old programs of who I am supposed to be*

Reframes

- *Place your hand over your heart chakra, the center of your chest as you repeat:*
- **Thank you, God, I am...**
- *Activating the energies of truth*
- *What is best for me is best for everyone.*
- *As I see the truth in myself I see the truth in others*
- *As I choose myself, I have more to give*
- *I make choices that are correct for me first*
- *As I think of myself first, and am sensitive to my own needs, I am clearer on how to support others in integrity*
- *God wants me to thrive and share my gifts with others*
- *There is no either/or, I am meant to experience both/and starting with myself*
- *It starts with me, and then extends to others*
- *I receive and then have more to give*
- *My true identity is already validated by God*

- *I am allowing pleasure and celebrating the pleasure of others*
- *I am comfortable with this new order of energy*
- *All is well*
- *Life is good*
- *I am blessed*

Take three deep breaths and fill yourself with light. Stand up and walk around to help ground these energies into your entire body.

Appendix 2

Resources to Support you in Mastering Affluence

Books by Carol Tuttle

Remembering Wholeness

It's Just My Nature

The Child Whisperer

Online Resources by Carol Tuttle

CarolTuttle.com

HealWithCarol.com

MyEnergyProfile.com

The30DayMoneyCure.com

DressingYourTruth.com

DYTMen.com (Dressing Your Truth for Men)

TheChildWhisperer.com

RememberingWholeness.com

MasteringAffluence.com

Online Courses by Carol Tuttle
Dressing Your Truth for Women
Dressing Your Truth for Men
The 30-Day Money Cure
Energy Profiling
The Carol Tuttle Healing Center

Healing Modalities Recommended by Carol
Emotional Freedom Technique, EFT or Tapping
Rapid Eye Therapy
Neuro Linguistic Programming, NLP

In a few places throughout this book, I mention or recommend my Energy Profiling System. Discovering which of the 4 Energy Types you express is a powerful tool in creating your affluent life. I offer a free online course to help you do this. I urge you to discover your Type for free at myenergyprofile.com.

On your way to a more affluent life, you may feel stuck by specific issues. Your challenge could be fear, weight, chronic health or money problems, lack of self-confidence, or long-term pain from childhood issues or abuse. I've created an extensive library of 100+ healing sessions and guided healing plans to support your unique needs. I'm here to help you heal and live the joyful life that calls to you. To learn more, visit healwithcarol.com.

Endnotes

i   *Dumb and Dumber*. Directed by Peter Farelly & Bobby Farelly. Warner Bros. Pictures, 1994.

ii   Michael Brown, *The Presence Process*, (New York: Beaufort Books, 2005).

iii   Carol Tuttle, *Remembering Wholeness*, (Seattle: Sea Script Company, 2000), page.

iv   Byron Katie, "The Work of Byron Katie." *Byron Katie International*, http://thework.com/en

v   Louise Hay, *You Can Heal Your Life*, (Hay House, 1984).

vi   "Positive Emotions and Your Health," *NIH News in Health*, August 2015, https://newsinhealth.nih.gov/2015/08/positive-emotions-your-health

vii   "Can Trauma Be Passed to Next Generation Through DNA?" *PBS Newshour*. August 31, 2015, http://www.pbs.org/newshour/extra/daily-videos/can-trauma-be-passed-to-next-generation-through-dna/

viii   Joe Dispenza, "What does the spike in the Schumann resonance mean?" *Dr. Joe Dispenza's Blog*, February 2017, https://www.drjoedispenza.com/blog/consciousness/what-does-the-spike-in-the-schumann-resonance-mean/

ix   *Groundhog Day.* Directed by Harold Ramis. Columbia Pictures Corporation, 1993.

x   Don Lincoln, "The Good Vibrations of Quantum Field Theories," *The Nature of Reality*, NOVA, August 5, 2013, http://www.pbs.org/wgbh/nova/blogs/physics/2013/08/the-good-vibrations-of-quantum-field-theories/

xi   Wayne Dyer, *The Power of Intention*, (Carlsbad: Hay House, 2004).

xii   M. Scott Peck, *The Road Less Traveled: A New Psychology of Love, Traditional Values and Spiritual Growth*, (Simon & Schuster, 1967).

xiii   "The Science of Healing Thoughts." Scientific American. January 19, 2016, https://www.scientificamerican.com/article/the-science-of-healing-thoughts/

xiv   Michael Pollan, *Food Rules: An Eater's Manual*, (New York: Penguin Group, 2009).

xv   Wally Minto, *The Results Book*, (Coleman Graphics, 1976).

xvi   P. M. Forni, Choosing Civility: *The Twenty Five Rules of Considerate Conduct*, (New York: St. Martin's Griffin, 2003).

xvii   Sheri Winston, *Women's Anatomy of Arousal*, (New York: Mango Garden Press, 2010).